A little course in...

Wine
Tasting

A little course in...

Wine
Tasting

DK

LONDON, NEW YORK, MUNICH, MELBOURNE, DELHI

Written by David Williams

Senior Editor Alastair Laing
Project Art Editor Gemma Fletcher
Managing Editor Penny Warren
Managing Art Editor Alison Donovan
Senior Jacket Creative Nicola Powling
Jacket Design Assistant Rosie Levine
Pre-production Producer Sarah Isle
Senior Producers Seyhan Esen, Jen Lockwood
Art Director Peter Luff, Jane Bull
Publisher Mary Ling

DK India
Art Editors Devan Das, Prashant Kumar
Senior Art Editor Ivy Roy
DTP Designers Rajesh Singh Adhikari, Sourabh Challariya
DTP Manager Sunil Sharma

Tall Tree Ltd
Editors Joe Fullman, Camilla Hallinan, Catherine Saunders
Designer Malcolm Parchment

First published in Great Britain in 2013 by
Dorling Kindersley Limited, 80 Strand, London WC2R 0RL
Penguin Group (UK)

2 4 6 8 10 9 7 5 3 1
001–187847–Jan/2013

A CIP catalogue record for this book is available
from the British Library.

ISBN 978 1 4093 6520 4

Printed and bound by Leo Paper Products Ltd, China

Discover more at
www.dk.com

Contents

Build Your Course 6 • How to Host a Wine Tasting 8
How to Choose the Right Glassware 10 • How to Serve Wine 12
The Science of... Growing Grapes 14 • Winemaking 16

1 Start Simple

2 Build On It

3 Take It Further

Build Your Course

This book is divided into three sections: Start Simple explores the range of flavours and aromas, and the main styles of wine. Build On It looks at famous grape varieties and classic styles produced across the world. Take It Further examines the wider factors that can affect wine, such as age or climate, and looks at how to match wine with food.

Getting started

Each section of the course is structured around a series of tutored tasting sessions. These tastings are designed to illustrate particular themes, and as you taste you will be learning about wine and developing your own palate at the same time. With each tasting, "Explore" pages first examine the theme of the tasting; these are followed by pages that introduce each of the wine styles selected for the tasting session; each

wine style then receives detailed tasting notes explaining what to expect from wines of this style and why; having picked your favourites, the session then concludes with buying advice and food pairings, and ideas for similar or contrasting wines to discover. Before you start to taste, whet your appetite with the introductory section where you'll find out how grapes are grown, how wine is produced, and how best to serve it.

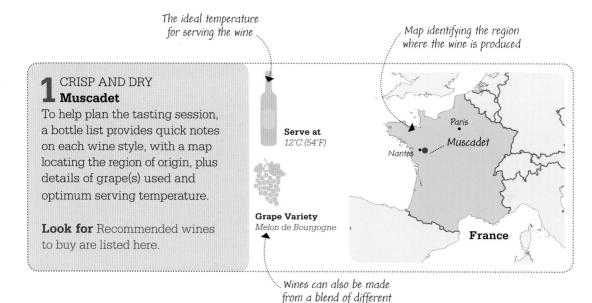

The ideal temperature for serving the wine

Map identifying the region where the wine is produced

1 CRISP AND DRY
Muscadet
To help plan the tasting session, a bottle list provides quick notes on each wine style, with a map locating the region of origin, plus details of grape(s) used and optimum serving temperature.

Look for Recommended wines to buy are listed here.

Serve at
12°C (54°F)

Grape Variety
Melon de Bourgogne

Paris

Muscadet

Nantes

France

Wines can also be made from a blend of different grape varieties

2 PINOT GRIGIO
Northeast Italy

Each wine has tasting notes interpreting the four key aspects of appearance, aroma, flavour, and texture

 Appearance can often be determined by the grape variety or winemaking method and each style has a unique colour.

 Aroma is an important and often very personal aspect of wine appreciation. What will you be able to detect?

Symbols represent the four aspects of tasting

 Flavour is closely linked to aroma and again, you might detect some unexpected notes in your wine.

Annotations help to explain wine labels

 Texture is surprisingly varied in wines, from light and subtle whites to heavy, viscous reds, with everything in between.

Livio Felluga
Pinot Grigio

3 FRANCE
Champagne

When you have learnt about the key wine styles, flavours, and areas of production, and developed a keener understanding of your own palate, it's time to use your knowledge.

Buying advice Recognise the best producers, get tips on what's value-for-money, and find out whether to drink young or lay down to mature.
Food pairing Get expert advice on what type of food will go best with each wine.
Also try If you like a particular wine in the tasting, be inspired to explore similar or contrasting wines and set up your own tastings.

By the time you finish this book you'll be toasting your wine expertise

How to Host a Wine Tasting

A fun way for you and your friends to get to know more about wine and explore the styles you like is to host a wine-tasting party. If you enjoy it, you can make it a regular event, choosing a different theme each time.

1 Choose a theme. The tasting sessions in this book are a great place to start and once you have tried them all you will be knowledgeable enough to devise your own themes. It could be based on season, geography, style, or something more quirky, but try to make it as focused as possible. Christmas, for example, is a great time to taste wines that you're likely to buy in for the season – Port or Champagne, perhaps. Or you could try wines from several different producers in a particular region that interests you, or a specific grape variety made in different regions around the world.

2 Invite your guests. To spread the cost, work, and fun, invite a group of friends (four to eight people or couples is a good number) and get them each to bring a bottle that fits in with the theme – making sure in advance that none of you bring the same bottle! It's also worth asking your guests to bring their own glasses, unless you already have a big collection and a good glass-washer.

For a truly "blind" and unbiased tasting, hide all traces of the brand

Reveal each wine's identity after your guests have finished their tasting notes

3 **Blind tasting.** Serving the wines "blind" – that is, with the bottles wrapped in paper and with all traces of the brand (foil capsules, corks, and screwcaps) hidden away – adds to the fun and focuses your mind on what you really like about the wine, not just its reputation or price. Once you've wrapped the bottles, label them clearly (A, B, C or 1, 2, 3 and so on).

4 **Explain the rules.** Before you start tasting, explain to everyone what they're drinking – "We have six classic European reds", for example. Provide pens and paper and get everyone to write down what they think of the wines, note their favourites, or even take a guess about where it might come from or how much it costs. Taste, drink, discuss, but do not reveal the wines until the end of the tasting, when all the guests are finished and ready.

5 **The results.** Ask your guests to hand you their notes and then reveal the bottles one by one, discussing each wine as you go. This is the time to see how the reality of the tasting matched up with each guest's expectations – did the famous brands and most expensive wines do the best? (You may be surprised at how often they don't.) Give your guests a chance to note down which wine is which, and then relax and enjoy your favourites.

Nibbles
Tasting wine is hungry work, and not much fun on an empty stomach. You'll need to provide some nibbles, but make sure the food is not too spicy or strong-tasting or it will overpower the wines.

GRAND VIN SEIGNEUR

Château
de
Haute-Serre

Appellation Cahors Contrôlée

Récolté sur les coteaux de Cahors

2003

GEORGES VIGOUROUX
Château à Cieurac - Lot
FRANCE
MIS EN BOUTEILLE AU CHÂTEAU

How to Choose the Right Glassware

Having the right glassware isn't just about making the table look
nice at a dinner party. Different wine styles work better with
different glass shapes and sizes, and using the right one
can greatly enhance your enjoyment.

...... *Pour to near
the top of
the glasss*

...... *Pour to
about a
third full*

...... *Pour to
about a
third full*

Flute

*Tall and narrow, these glasses
leave just a small surface area
on top of the wine, making
them suitable for conserving
bubbles in fizzy wines.*

Crisp white wine glass

*Larger than the flute, but still
quite small and narrow, this glass
keeps the wine cool and shows
off the acidity and delicate
flavours of crisp white wines.*

Full-bodied white wine glass

*A wider opening allows for more
contact with the air to bring out
the complex flavours of rich dry
whites, but the glass is still small
enough to keep the wine cool.*

"The right glassware not only looks great but helps the wine taste better."

...... Pour to about a third full

...... Pour a third to half full

...... Pour to just over half full

Burgundy glass
A large surface area is left in contact with the air, but the top of the glass tapers in to keep the subtle, delicate aromas of elegant reds in the glass.

Bordeaux glass
Again, a large surface area exposes the wine to the air, allowing big, robust, rich red wines plenty of room to release their complex aromas.

Dessert wine glass
A smaller glass suits the smaller servings of sweeter wines, usually poured at the end of a meal, and keeps the wine cool.

How to Serve Wine

When it comes to serving wine, the most important thing to consider is temperature. Each style works best at a different temperature. If in doubt, remember: cooler is better, since a glass can always warm up at the table.

Using an ice bucket
Add water to ice cubes: it works faster because the icy liquid has a greater contact area with the bottle than ice cubes alone.

Take care when opening your bubbly!

Crisp whites and bubbly
These styles of wine are all about refreshment, and as with other thirst-quenching drinks, refreshment works best cold. Serve them straight from the fridge or ice bucket at 6–8°C (43–46°F).

25°C (77°F)
20°C (68°F)
15°C (59°F)
10°C (50°F)
5°C (41°F)
0°C (32°F)

Rich whites, rosés, and dessert and fortified wines
A little bit of chill helps keep these wines fresh; too much will inhibit your appreciation of their rich texture and aroma. Take them from the fridge 20 minutes before serving at 10–12°C (50–54°F).

25°C (77°F)
20°C (68°F)
15°C (59°F)
10°C (50°F)
5°C (41°F)
0°C (32°F)

How to Decant

Decanting wine from the bottle is a way of allowing oxygen into the wine to soften the tannin and acidity and to help the wine release its complex aromas. It is also used for old red wines where harmless sediment has formed at the bottom of the bottle.

Splash
Pour the wine into the decanter from as a high a point as you can, allowing it splash on the inside of the decanter.

Swirl
Supporting it with one hand at the bottom, carefully swirl the decanter, allowing as much air into the wine as possible.

Light reds

Red wines are often served unchilled, but lighter styles (see pp.52–53) work better with a little time in the fridge – 20–30 minutes / 12–14°C (54–57°F) – to accentuate their refreshing character.

25°C (77°F)
20°C (68°F)
15°C (59°F)
10°C (50°F)
5°C (41°F)
0°C (32°F)

Rich reds and vintage port

For full-bodied reds, room temperature made sense when homes were cooler. Aim for 16–18°C (61–64°F); any cooler inhibits their complex flavours and textures; warmer will make them soupy.

25°C (77°F)
20°C (68°F)
15°C (59°F)
10°C (50°F)
5°C (41°F)
0°C (32°F)

The science of **Growing Grapes**

A year in the life of a vineyard can be hugely rewarding and also highly stressful. At the mercy of the elements, growers must reckon with heavy rain, strong winds, frost, and hail, as well as the pests and diseases that can threaten a harvest. With careful planning, plenty of nurturing, and a little luck, however, the seasonal journey may just produce a truly great vintage.

Early spring As temperatures rise, new buds begin to break on the vines. Different grape varieties will bud at different times, depending on the weather conditions and soil type. Frost, pests, and diseases are the main concerns at this stage.

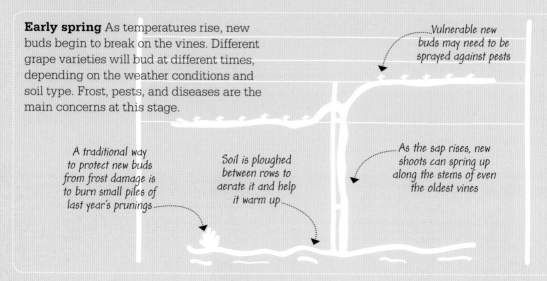

Vulnerable new buds may need to be sprayed against pests

A traditional way to protect new buds from frost damage is to burn small piles of last year's prunings

Soil is ploughed between rows to aerate it and help it warm up

As the sap rises, new shoots can spring up along the stems of even the oldest vines

Late spring Over the course of 10 days or so in late spring, the vines will burst into flower. This is a stressful time for growers, as bad weather can kill off the flowers and inhibit pollinating insects. Sunshine and a light breeze offer perfect conditions for pollination.

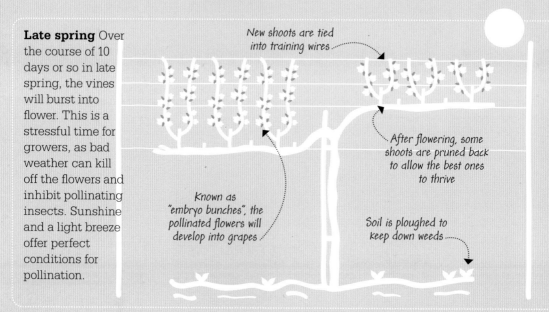

New shoots are tied into training wires

Known as "embryo bunches", the pollinated flowers will develop into grapes

After flowering, some shoots are pruned back to allow the best ones to thrive

Soil is ploughed to keep down weeds

Summer The embryo bunches are now growing into recognizable grapes, attracting hungry birds in the process. Growers can improve their harvest by removing some bunches so that others can better develop. This is known as a "green harvest".

The "green harvest" reduces the crop, but improves its quality

Vines must be netted to prevent birds from consuming the young grapes

Pruning allows more air and sunlight to reach the remaining crop

Autumn When the grapes have ripened and red grapes changed colour, they can be harvested. This is usually in early autumn, though timings can vary depending on the weather. Once they have been harvested, the soil is then fertilized and ploughed.

White grapes are harvested before black, to preserve higher acidity

Mature grapes will be plump and full tint

Pressed grape skins left over from winemaking can be used as fertilizer

Harvested grapes ready to go to the winery for processing

Winter During the cold winter months the vines are dormant. As the sap stops flowing, any grapes left on the vine dehydrate or freeze, which enhances their sugar content. Such grapes, and those affected by botrytis ("noble rot") are ideal for making sweet or ice wines.

When dormant, leaves drop and sap retreats to protect the vine from the cold

Remaining grapes that have rotted or frozen can be used to make sweet wine

If all grapes have been picked, stems are pruned back to prepare for spring buds

The soil is ploughed to protect the vine roots from frost

The science of **Winemaking**

White, red or rosé, still or sparkling; all wine is the product of the same basic process of crushing and pressing grapes to extract the juice, and then fermenting the juice with yeast to produce alcohol. Knowing how wine is made will help you better understand how different elements of the winemaking process can affect the taste and quality of a wine.

WHITE WINE PROCESS

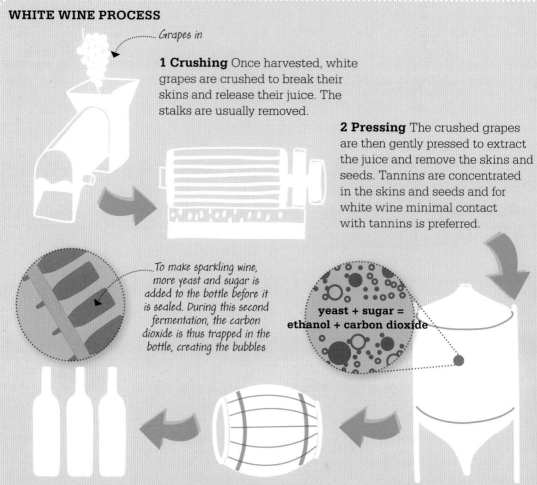

Grapes in

1 Crushing Once harvested, white grapes are crushed to break their skins and release their juice. The stalks are usually removed.

2 Pressing The crushed grapes are then gently pressed to extract the juice and remove the skins and seeds. Tannins are concentrated in the skins and seeds and for white wine minimal contact with tannins is preferred.

To make sparkling wine, more yeast and sugar is added to the bottle before it is sealed. During this second fermentation, the carbon dioxide is thus trapped in the bottle, creating the bubbles

yeast + sugar = ethanol + carbon dioxide

5 Bottling Preservatives like sulphur dioxide are added to prevent fermentation in the bottle. The wine is then filtered, bottled, and sealed with a cork or synthetic cap.

4 Maturation After 1–2 weeks, the liquid can be racked, leaving behind the dead yeast and other sediments (lees). It can be stored in oak barrels to mature or bottled immediately.

3 Fermentation The addition of yeast triggers fermentation, converting the glucose (sugar) in the juice to ethanol (alcohol), and releasing carbon dioxide, which escapes into the air.

RED WINE PROCESS

1 Crushing Red or black grapes are crushed to break the skins and release their juices. About 60–70% of the grapes' juice is extracted at this stage, known as free-run juice.

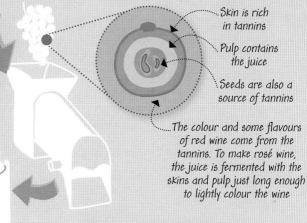

Skin is rich in tannins

Pulp contains the juice

Seeds are also a source of tannins

The colour and some flavours of red wine come from the tannins. To make rosé wine, the juice is fermented with the skins and pulp just long enough to lightly colour the wine

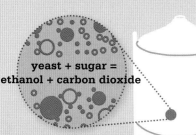

yeast + sugar = ethanol + carbon dioxide

2 First fermentation The crushed grapes, skins, and free-run juice are fermented with yeast, which converts the sugar to ethanol (alcohol) and carbon dioxide.

3 Pressing After first fermentation, the must (pulp) and skins are pressed to extract all the remaining juice and as much colour and flavour from the tannins as desired. This is called press wine.

malic acid + bacteria = lactic acid + carbon dioxide

5 Maturation After 3–6 months, the wine can be racked to remove the lees and clarify the liquid. The wine may then be placed in oak barrels to mature, or bottled immediately.

6 Bottling Preservatives are added to protect against bacteria and oxidization. The wine is then filtered, to remove particles and microbes, and bottled and sealed.

4 Second fermentation Free-run wine (unpressed) and press wine can be mixed, before undergoing bacterial fermentation. This process converts malic acid into lactic acid, for a milder flavour.

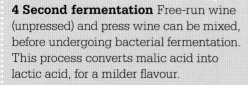

1

Start simple

It's time to start the practical part of this course, and when it comes to learning about wine, the good news is that "practical" means opening some bottles and drinking! In this section we'll be looking at the basic differences between wines, helping you to find out which styles best suit your palate.

In this section, learn about:

Key Taste Areas
pp.20–23

Flavours and Aromas
pp.24–29

How to Taste Wine
pp.30–37

White Wine Styles
pp.38–47

Red Wine Styles
pp.48–57

Rosé Wine Styles
pp.58–63

Explore

The Key Taste Areas of Wine

Wine is an experience that calls on all of your senses. Your senses of smell and taste do the work when it comes to flavour, of course. But just looking at a wine can tell you a great deal about where it comes from and how it is made. And texture, too – the way the wine feels in your mouth – is an enormous part of wine's appeal.

Getting in touch with your senses

Almost 80% of the flavours we taste come through the olfactory receptors in our nose. On its own, the tongue is only capable of tasting bitterness, sweetness, saltiness, and sourness. It is the nose that enables us to taste all the complex flavours of wine.

The spectrum of flavours in wine is so vast, and people's individual perception of taste varies so greatly, it is hard to imagine a clear and consistent vocabulary capable of describing so many nuances. All wines, however, can be broken down into a set of components that stimulate your tongue in different ways. Being able to identify the intensity of each component in the wines that you like is the first step on the road to becoming a discriminating wine taster.

Sweetness

Sweetness (and fruitiness) is all about the level of grape sugar in the wine. Wines are made with differing levels of sugar, from dry (technically less than 4g / 0.1 oz of sugar per litre) to very sweet (50g / 1.75 oz or more).

Acidity

The presence of acidity in wine is what makes it refreshing. The more acidity a wine contains, the more your tongue and palate will feel stimulated, for what is literally a mouthwatering experience.

Tannins

Tannins are natural chemicals found in grape pips and skins – as well as in tea and tree bark – that give wines, particularly red wines, a mouth-drying astringency. This astringency can be felt not only across the tongue but also on the teeth.

Alcohol and weight

The result of the grape sugar undergoing fermentation during the winemaking process, alcohol is what gives body and weight to a wine. A wine with higher alcohol content will feel fuller or heavier on the tongue than a wine with lower alcohol. Excessive alcohol in a wine can give an unpleasant burning sensation, particularly at the back of the throat as you swallow.

Building blocks *These two diagrams show at a glance the key components that different wines will balance in all sorts of different ways.*

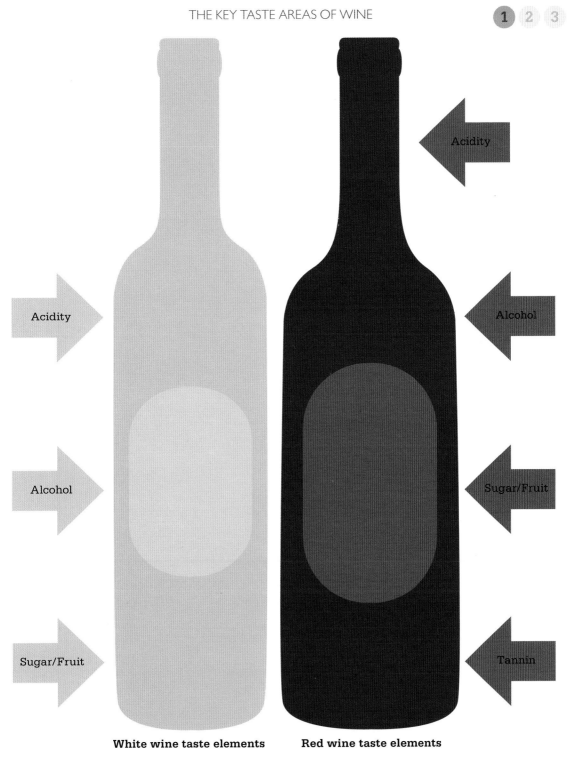

Acidity

Acidity

Alcohol

Alcohol

Sugar/Fruit

Sugar/Fruit

Tannin

White wine taste elements   **Red wine taste elements**

Taste Test

This is a fun way of easing yourself into the world of wine tasting. The idea is to practise spotting the key taste and textural qualities that are found in wine.

Acidity

Take five glasses of similar size. Half-fill four of them with tap or mineral water. Now squeeze the juice of a large lemon into a jug. Add about a third of the juice to one of the glasses of water and the rest to another glass. Then squeeze another lemon, and add it all to a third glass of water. Next, squeeze the juice of a whole lemon into the empty glass. Leave the final glass of water as it is.

Take a sip from each glass, starting with the plain water and moving through the weakest solution to the pure lemon juice, each time allowing the liquid to circulate around your mouth before swallowing.

As you taste, pay particular attention to how your tongue and gums *feel*. The stronger the solution, the higher the acidity, and the more your mouth will feel stimulated – it will feel, literally, mouthwatering.

Sweetness

Now put the glasses of lemon solution to one side, remembering which glass contains which strength, and pour yourself four more half-glasses of water. Add half a teaspoon of white caster sugar to the first glass, a teaspoonful to the second glass, two teaspoons to the third, and four teaspoons to the fourth. Give each glass a good stir until the sugar is fully dissolved.

Now repeat the procedure you used with the lemon solutions, tasting your way through each of the sugar solutions, starting with the glass of water and then moving from the weakest to the strongest, each time allowing the liquid to circulate around your mouth before swallowing

Again, which glass – which level of sweetness – do you prefer?

Tannin

For the third taste component, put a tea bag into each of four mugs. Add boiling water and brew the tea in each mug to different strengths: the first mug for 10 seconds, the second for 30 seconds, the third for a minute, and the fourth for five minutes.

Allow the tea to cool and then pour into four glasses. Taste each in turn, from the weakest to the strongest, this time paying attention to the texture of the liquid all over your tongue and teeth. The stronger the tea, the more astringent and drying it will feel – this is caused by tannin, one of the key components of tea and red wine.

Alcohol

For the final taste component, take four glasses and add a single-measure of vodka to each. Mix increasing levels of water to three of the four glasses – doubling the amount of water as you move across. Leave the fourth glass neat.

Once again, take a good sip and swill around your mouth. Notice the effects on your tongue and throat: the higher the strength, the more you will feel a sensation of "heat".

Mix and match

To finish this taste test, try mixing up the different tea, sugar, and lemon solutions. The more lemon you mix with the sweet solution, for example, the less prominent the acidity feels. Likewise, adding sweetness and acidity to the strong tea makes the solution feel much less astringent. This is the same in wine, where balance between the components is everything.

More of a challenge

Once you have tasted your way through the different glasses, ask a friend to mix up the order and blindfold you. Now have a go at guessing which concentration of lemon, sugar, tea, or vodka each glass contains. Think also about which of those concentrations is most pleasing to you. Some people have a higher tolerance for acidity, others a sweet tooth – which are you?

Moving to wine

As a last step, pour yourself a glass of wine – it doesn't matter what colour, brand, or style you choose, any wine will do. Take a sip and think about those taste elements again. Does the wine taste sweet? How much acidity does it have? What about tannin? And does it leave a feeling of heat on the finish? If you can pinpoint these elements in the wine you have started to develop your wine palate.

Explore

The Range of Flavours and Aromas in Wine

In a sense, the last tasting was a warm-up for the mouth and dealt with how wine feels. Now we're going to exercise the nose, which is largely responsible for how wine tastes.

The language of wine

There's no doubt that, to the uninitiated, one of the more off-putting things about wine is the language used to describe it. As in other areas of expertise, such as modern art and haute couture, there is always the sneaking suspicion that wine talk is all rather pretentious, snooty, and only distantly related to the reality of what is in the glass. It's a popular misconception that was perhaps best summed up in a famous New Yorker cartoon, where the character says of a wine: "It's a domestic Burgundy without any breeding, but I'm sure you'll be amused by its presumption."

Don't be put off

For those who really love wine, however, to describe wine is not to enter a competition to see who can find the most outlandish description and alienate the most people. Most words used to describe wine – even words that might seem the most fanciful such as sweat, tar, or wet stone – are chosen because the wine really does taste like that. Take cat's pee, for example, which might sound off-putting but is routinely associated with wonderful wines made from the Sauvignon Blanc grape variety for sound reasons: many Sauvignon Blancs contain a chemical compound similar to that found in the feline emission. Less startling descriptions such as blackcurrant and roses are also based on chemical compounds found in both the wine and the thing with which it's being compared.

Making wine memorable

The real benefit of describing a wine's flavours and aromas is that it helps you remember that wine, fixing it in your mind to be stored away for your next buying mission. Over the next few pages, we'll take a look at some of the most common flavours and aromas found in wine. If you have a bottle to hand, why not open it up, pour yourself a glass, and see which flavours you can spot? Or why not warm up for wine tasting by gathering as many as possible of the fruits, spices, and other originals listed on pp.26–29 and reminding yourself of their aromas and flavours?

Lemons and other citrus fruit *have memorable flavours and aromas that are often found in wines.*

White and Sparkling Flavours/Aromas

A vast range of flavours and aromas can be found in white wines, both still and sparkling. Familiarize yourself with some of the most common and see if you can spot them the next time you have a glass of wine.

Citrus

Lemon, Grapefruit, Orange, Lime *Citrus flavours are often found in crisp, refreshing, dry white wines and sparkling wines.*

Orchard

Plum, Peach, Apple, Pear, Quince, Apricot *Some grape varieties produce specific aromas – peaches are characteristic in Viognier (see pp.44 and 151) and Albariño (see p.97), for example.*

Tropical

Melon, Mango, Pineapple, Banana, Lychee, Guava *Typical in white wines from warmer climates. Often found in rich and sweet dessert wines (see p.46).*

Green

Grass, Green Pepper, Nettles, Hay, Herbs, Artichokes, Green Beans, Fennel *Wines made from the Sauvignon Blanc (see p.71) grape variety are renowned for their green character.*

Floral

Acacia Flowers, White Flowers, Honeysuckle, Roses, Geraniums *Riesling (see p.72) is often floral when young.*

Others

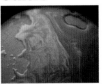

Petrol, Sweat, Cat's Pee *Strange but true!*

Nutty

Almonds, Hazelnuts *Older whites often take on nutty flavours.*

Wood

Oak, Cedar Wood, Sandalwood *Some white wines are aged in oak barrels, imparting woody characters.*

Spice

Cinnamon, Cloves, Ginger, White Pepper *Some grape varieties give spicy flavours: Grüner Veltliner (see p.98) often has white pepper, for example.*

Mineral

Wet Stones, Salt, Steel *Elusive and often a sign of quality.*

Bakery shop

Honey, Brioche, Vanilla, Butter, Toast, Yeast, Biscuits, Butterscotch, Toffee, Chocolate, Dried Fruit, Raisins *Found in rich white wines and quality sparkling wines.*

Red and Rosé Flavours/Aromas

Some flavours and aromas are common to red, rosé, and white wines, but the fruit character of reds is usually darker than in whites. Some wines charm by tasting very strongly of one character; the best wines are usually complex combinations of many.

Citrus

Blood Orange, Pink Grapefruit, Mandarin *Citrus characters are frequently found in Pinot Noir (see pp.85 and 126) and Sangiovese wines (see p.109).*

Red Fruit and Vegetables

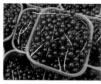 

Redcurrant, Strawberry, Cranberry, Raspberry, Red Cherry, Red Plum, Tomato, Beetroot *Rosés and lighter reds usually have more of a red-fruit character.*

Black Fruit

Blueberry, Blackberry, Dark Plum, Blackcurrant, Damson, Mulberry *Black fruit is the most common description for red wines of all styles.*

Dried Fruit

Prune, Raisin, Fig *Reds produced in warmer climates (see p.153) often have a dried-fruit character.*

Floral

Violets, Roses, Jasmine *The Nebbiolo grape variety often has a rose bouquet.*

Savoury

Balsamic Vinegar, Bacon, Olives, Black Pepper, Mushrooms, Truffles, Game *These savoury characters tend to emerge in older wines.*

Green

Geen Pepper, Mint, Tomato Leaf, Peapod, Herbs, Eucalyptus, Fennel, Aniseed *May be a sign of unripe grapes, but can add a leafy freshness.*

Café

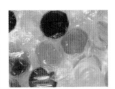

Chocolate, Boiled Sweets, Tobacco, Coffee, Tea, Toast, Vanilla, Coconut, Kola Nut *Many of these aromas come through ageing the wine in oak barrels (see p.145).*

Other

Tar, Pencil Lead, Leather, Smoke, Bubblegum *Tar is often found in Syrah from France's Rhône Valley (see p.108); bubblegum is linked to the winemaking process carbonic maceration.*

Wood

Oak, Cedar Wood, Acacia Wood *The result of ageing a wine in oak barrels.*

Mineral

Wet Stones, Iron *As in white wines, elusive but often a sign of high quality.*

29

Explore

How to Taste Wine

The real objective with wine is to enjoy drinking it, rather than just twirling the glass and sniffing the contents. However, if you want to develop informed tastes, that requires a certain amount of connoisseurship.

Tasting to some purpose

Being a connoisseur doesn't mean becoming a wine snob; a "connoisseur" simply knows their subject. The best way to get to know wine, and to understand your own likes and dislikes, is to taste wine thoughtfully rather than merely swallowing it. By examining, savouring, contemplating, and even discussing your wine, instead of just drinking it, you will learn how to use your senses to evaluate the wine and form an opinion of it. There are some key areas to focus on when tasting wine. Colour: is it light in colour, suggesting a light taste too? As they age, reds go from bright purple or ruby to a brick-like colour. Whites take on a deeper, more golden hue as they mature. Viscosity: heavy drip lines or "legs" in the glass indicate viscosity, which gives you a clue about how weighty the wine will feel in the mouth. Smell: think back to the aromas on pp.26–9. Can you spot any? Think about what you smell to help you remember a wine or relate it to similar wines in the future. Flavour: after smelling, try to analyse what you can taste. Does it taste good? Great wines tend to have complex flavours that hang together in balance.

The four basic steps of wine tasting are described opposite: try practising them on the four main types of wine that follow.

Pour a glass *of your chosen wine, and let the tasting process commence.*

1 Gripping the glass by its stem, hold it at an angle in front of a piece of white paper or a white tablecloth so you can examine the colour. Study the wine. What does the colour tell you about it?

2 Swirl the wine carefully to coat the sides of the glass and release a stronger aroma. Smell deeply by putting your nose into the glass and slowly inhaling. What can you smell?

3 Take a good-sized sip of the wine and concentrate on its flavours. Does it taste like it smells? Maybe even better? Can you taste new flavours? Are they pleasant, or unpleasantly intrusive?

4 Feel the wine's texture. Sense its viscosity in your mouth. Take time to savour the finish. A good quality wine's flavour lingers in your mouth after swallowing; great wines have long finishes.

1 TASTING
White Wine

Appearance White wines are transparent and range from pale, almost watery to greenish-yellow, straw-yellow, and gold.

White wines are almost always made from grapes with green and yellow skins.

Aroma and flavour There is a huge range of aromas and flavours in white wine (see pp.26–7). Whatever

their character, they tend to be more delicate than in red wines.

This delicacy comes down to the winemaking process – the juice for white wines has much less contact with the grape skins than the juice for reds, which means fewer of the flavour compounds found in the grape skins (and known as phenolics) are extracted.

Texture Although white wines range from the very light to the very rich, and from the dry to the very sweet, they should always feel refreshing.

The crisp and refreshing quality of all good white wines, whether dry, gently sweet, or lusciously rich, comes from ensuring there is enough acidity in the grapes when they are harvested.

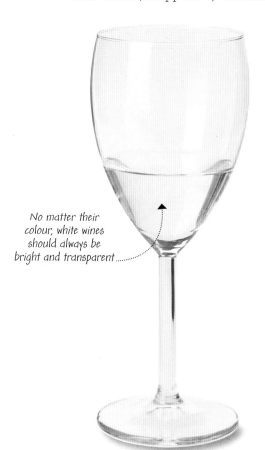

No matter their colour, white wines should always be bright and transparent

"*White wines range in style, but generally feel lighter and more delicate than reds.*"

2 TASTING Red Wine

 Appearance Red wines can range from brick-like to ruby red to violet and dark purple. They can be translucent and pale, or dark and inky, almost opaque.

Red wines are made from black grapes, and their colour comes from the pigment in the grape skin; the precise hue depends on grape variety, winemaking techniques, and the age of the wine.

Holding a glass of wine to the light over a piece of white paper is a good way of showing off its colour

  Aroma and flavour The fruit aromas and flavours of red wine are darker in character than in white wines: red and black fruits such as cherries, berries, plums, currants, dried dark fruit, and jam, rather than citrus, orchard, or tropical fruit (see pp.28–9).

These darker fruits are the result of the flavour compounds found in the skin cells of black grapes, which are released during the complex process of fermentation. The precise fruit character depends on where the fruit is grown, the grape variety used, and the amount of sun and warmth it has received.

 Texture The drying, chewy sensation around the teeth and gums is a key distinction between a red wine and a white.

This sensation is caused by tannin, most of which comes from the skins, pips, and stems of grapes (and from the oak barrels some wines are aged in). Because the juice stays in contact with those elements longer in red winemaking than it does with white and rosé, red wines are far higher in tannins.

"Red wine is more robust and astringent than white."

3 TASTING Rosé Wine

 Appearance Rosés range from very pale onion-skin to cherry red to a bright, almost luminous pink.

Rosé wines are usually made by gently pressing black grapes, leaving the juice in contact with the skins for just a short time before separating it and fermenting it like a white wine (see pp.16–17).

 Aroma Fresh and fruity, with delicate red fruit such as strawberries, raspberries, cherries, and cranberries.

Some rosés are made with a little sweetness, some are bone-dry; they should have the aromatic delicacy of a white wine but with the fruit spectrum of a lighter red.

 Flavour Zesty and fresh citrus alongside subtle red fruit.

Try tasting a white wine and a rosé while blindfolded. Pale, dry rosé wines often taste and feel like a crisp, dry white wine in the mouth, with lots of citrusy characters – can you spot the difference?

 Texture Light and crisp. Refreshing, delicate. Darker styles tend to feel weightier in the mouth, and may even have a little tannin.

As with their taste, when it comes to texture, most rosé wines feel like whites in the mouth, thanks to the absence of tannin and the crisp, fresh feeling.

The colour of rosé comes from the black grapes' skins

"Think of rosé wines as white wines made from red grapes: they are delicate, refreshing, and fun."

4 TASTING
Sparkling Wine

Appearance Whether it's red, rosé, or, by far the most common, white, a sparkling wine is of course marked out by its bubbles.

Sparkling wines generally get their bubbles by a process known as secondary fermentation (see p.16), which can take place in individual bottles or in a tank, or by the injection of carbon dioxide.

Aromas and flavours Sparkling wines often have aromas of baked bread, brioche, and biscuits.

The distinctive "patisserie" shop aromas of some sparkling wines are the result of the wine resting in contact with the dead yeast cells (lees) after the fizz-providing secondary fermentation.

Texture The bubbles can feel soft and creamy, fine and tingling, or fat and spiky. Underneath the bubbles, the wine will usually feel light, crisp, and fresh.

The texture of the bubbles is one way of gauging the quality of a sparkling wine: the softer and finer they are, the better the quality; carbonated wines will generally give a spiky, aggressive feel.

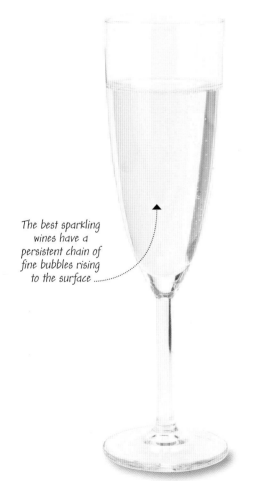

The best sparkling wines have a persistent chain of fine bubbles rising to the surface

"*Sparkling wines come in all colours, and are distinguished by their appetizing bubbles.*"

Understanding Differences Between Wines

As a fun way to complete this taste test, why not try doing it blind? Try guess which style is which without looking first, paying particular attention to the texture or feel of the wine.

1 WHITE WINE
Generally more delicate in flavour and texture, and without the drying texture of tannin found in red wine, many people find white wines more accessible when they begin their vinous journey of discovery. White wines are usually made from white grapes (with green-to-yellow skins), but in some cases from gently pressed black grapes (see p.74). They can be dry (very little sugar left in the wine after winemaking) or sweet, with a range of styles in between.

Fresh, crisp with delicate flavours and a lighter texture than reds.

2 RED WINE
More powerful in flavour and feeling heavier in the mouth than white wines, red wines also contain more tannins than white wines, which give them a drying feel like strongly brewed tea. They are always made from black grapes (with red-to-purple skins), although very occasionally there may also be some white grapes included. They can be sweet, but most widely available red wines are dry.

Denser and more powerful than whites, with tannin and darker fruit flavours.

3 ROSÉ WINE
Halfway between red and white wine, both in colour (ranging from pale onion-skin to very dark pink) and in flavour profile and texture, rosé wines taste fresher, more delicate, and much less drying on the palate than red wines, and have very little tannin. Rosé wines are made with black grapes, but with much shorter contact between the juice and the skins during winemaking. Most rosés are either dry or off-dry.

Lighter than reds, fresh like whites, a mix of red and citrus fruits.

4 SPARKLING WINE
Fizzy wines are made by taking still wines of any colour (but usually white), and adding or creating bubbles by a secondary winemaking process (see p.16). They are usually made in a fresh, crisp style with higher acidity than white or red wines. Although sparkling wines usually taste dry, they often contain more sugar than red or white wine, but the sweetness of the sugar is often masked by the wine's acidity.

Bubbles are the main difference – they should feel fresh and crisp.

In a blind test *you will probably spot the sparkling wine but can you taste which is white, red, or rosé?*

Explore

White Wine Styles

Breaking wine down by style – rather than by country of origin
or grape variety – makes what can come across as a complicated
subject so much easier to understand and explore. In this section
we'll be exploring the five main styles of white wine.

Flavour signposts

There are thousands of white wines made all over the world each year, but most of them fit into five broad categories, or styles. The categories are by no means mutually exclusive – they are more like signposts on a road that goes from the very palest, driest, and lightest wines to the richest and sweetest, and many wines straddle two categories. But thinking about wine in this way is the best means of getting you to think about and understand what you like, and why.

The styles

The first category, dry and crisp, covers wines that are deliberately light and subtle. They are all about refreshment and make great accompaniments to seafood. The wines of the next group, fruity and dry, are also highly refreshing, but they have a little more obvious fruit flavour, and may feel a bit heavier or fuller in the mouth. Rich and dry whites, meanwhile, are the heavyweights of dry white wine, with a full texture in the mouth that is sometimes described as opulent. These are joined by the sweeter styles: off-dry whites are those that have just a little sweetness alongside their aromatic flavours; rich sweet whites are the golden, sticky, luscious wines that work best with desserts.

Mood and food

In this tasting we'll be looking at five wines that are benchmark examples of each style. If there is a style you like, why not go out and look for wines of the same style? Equally, as you taste, think about when you might drink each style. Wine is no different from food in this respect: just as some days you'll want a burger and other days pizza or sushi, so each style is suited to a different food, occasion, or even mood.

White wine styles run the gamut from light and subtle to thick and opulent.

Tasting Session

1 CRISP AND DRY
Muscadet
A bone-dry white wine from the area around Nantes in the western Loire that is commonly consumed with the abundant local seafood.

Look for Fief Guérin Muscadet Côtes de Grandlieu Sur Lie, Loire. Or try a Muscadet-sur-Lie from Domaine de L'écu

Serve at
12°C (54°F)

Grape Variety
Melon de Bourgogne

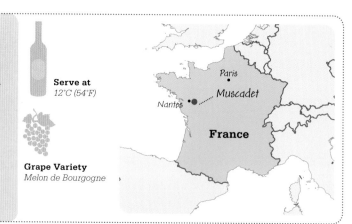

2 FRUITY AND DRY
Rueda
A pungently fruity dry white made largely from the K-naia Verdejo grape variety in Rueda in the northwestern Spanish province of Castilla y Léon.

Look for Palacio de Bornos Verdejo, one of the most popular white wines in Spain; K-naia Verdejo

Serve at
12°C (54°F)

Grape Varieties
Verdejo, Viura, Sauvignon Blanc

---

3 RICH AND DRY
Australian Viognier
Viognier is a grape variety that originated in France's Rhône Valley but has been enthusiastically embraced in the past ten years by wine producers around the world.

Look for Yalumba Eden Valley Viognier; The Lane Black Label Viognier

Serve at
14°C (57°F)

Grape Variety
Viognier

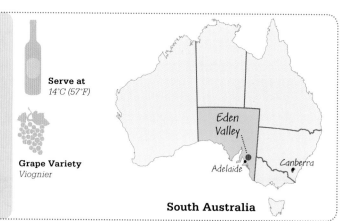

4 GENTLY SWEET
Riesling

The Riesling grape variety is often used for dry wines, but some winemakers in Germany, Alsace, and New Zealand frequently make it in a delicate, slightly sweet style.

Look for Dr L Riesling, Mosel Germany; Forrest The Doctors' Riesling, Marlborough New Zealand

Serve at
12°C (54°F)

Grape Variety
Riesling

Bernkastel-Kues

Berlin

Germany

Frankfurt

5 RICH AND SWEET
Sauternes

The Sauternes region of Bordeaux in France makes some of the world's finest, most luscious, golden sweet wines.

Look for For affordable Sauternes try Cyprès de Climens from top producer Château Climens, or Les Lions de Suduiraut

Serve at
13°C (55°F)

Grape Varieties
Sauvignon Blanc, Sémillon, Muscadelle

• Paris

France

Bordeaux
Barsac

These typical Alsace houses are found in Strasbourg, near the German border, at the heart of the Riesling wine region.

1 CRISP AND DRY
Muscadet

Appearance Very pale lemon yellow with a touch of green.

Crisp dry whites are usually made from grapes with large berries and thin skins in cooler climates, giving them less colour than richer wines.

Aroma A subtle mix of lemony citrus fruit, green apples, and pears. Not very intense.

The delicate aromas of dry crisp whites are easy to miss if you're used to strong flavours. But bear with them – it's part of their charm.

Flavour Fresh lemon-and-apple fruit, a slight salty, yeasty tang.

Crisp dry whites are designed to be refreshing accompaniments to light food; their flavours should complement rather than overwhelm the dish.

Texture Very dry, lightweight, and with a bright, clean but not tart, citrus-like acidity.

Made from early-ripening grapes that must be picked early to retain their acidity, crisp dry whites have a refreshing lemony tang. The best wines of this style always feel very dry and fresh as soon as they hit the tongue – but they shouldn't feel tart or sour.

"Clean as a whistle with lemon-citrus tang."

The best-quality Muscadets have sur lie on the label

2 FRUITY AND DRY
Rueda

Palacio de Bornos has vineyards in some of the best sites in the Spanish region of Rueda ....

Appearance Pale straw with a touch of green.

The colour suggests this wine has been made from grapes grown in a relatively cool, temperate climate (Rueda's vineyards benefit from their relatively high altitude).

Aroma Much more intensely aromatic than Muscadet. Pungent grapefruit, peaches, melon; a slight (not unpleasant) sweatiness.

Fruity aromatic whites express the naturally aromatic grape varieties used to make them (in this case, Verdejo).

Flavour Zesty, fresh fruit with zingy grapefruit, peach, and tropical fruit. Dry.

This is the taste of the Verdejo grape, which, like most fruity dry whites, is fermented at cool temperatures in stainless steel tanks to preserve the delicate fruit flavours.

Texture In a word, juicy. Though more rounded, generous, and weighty than the Muscadet, it doesn't feel heavy, and it finishes dry and clean.

Fruity dry whites have a similar texture to crisp dry whites and work with similar foods.

3 RICH AND DRY
Australian Viognier

 Appearance Bright yellow to rich gold.

Many rich full dry whites are aged in oak barrels, where the subtle influence of oxygen brings a golden hue.

 Aroma Compared with the previous two wines, the fruit is warmer: very ripe peaches and apricots, and a touch of honeysuckle.

Rich, full, dry whites often hail from warmer climates where the fruit develops much more sugar and flavour compounds, leading to a richer, more robust aroma.

 Flavour Opulent flavours of ripe peaches, honeysuckle, and pears.

Compared with both the crisp dry white and the fruity dry white, again the sense is of much riper fruit, almost falling off the tree.

 Texture Weighty in the mouth, perhaps even a little fat and viscous. No matter how rich it feels, however, a good rich dry white will always finish clean and dry.

This style of wine uses small-berried, thick-skinned grapes which produce less juice than those used for crisp white wines, but with more concentration and weight. Rich dry whites are generally higher in alcohol, again because they are made from ripe grapes containing more sugar, and this also gives more body to the wine.

South Australia's Yalumba winery is a specialist in the Viognier grape variety

4 GENTLY SWEET
Riesling

 Appearance Off-dry whites run the gamut of white-wine colours from pale silver-white (like the Riesling tasted here) to bright gold.

You cannot tell from sight alone if a wine is going to be sweet.

 Aroma The wine in this tasting has a nose of white flowers, subtle peach, and apple. But gently sweet white wines come with all kinds of fruit characters and intensity.

Again, you cannot tell if a wine is sweet or dry from the nose. Even this style of lightly aromatic Riesling can be made in a dry style.

 Flavour In this wine, a touch of sweetness is just discernible behind subtle apple, peach, and zesty, mouthwatering lime, with a hint of steel or mineral flavours.

That little touch of sweetness is the key to this style of wine, which can include examples of all the other styles of white wines. You can find crisp, light wines which have this sweet touch. You can find fruity aromatic whites such as this Riesling. Even some rich whites will sometimes be made with a little sugar.

 Texture This Riesling has a delicate feel – it's light in alcohol but it doesn't feel sticky or sickly.

That is the key to successful off-dry styles. The little bit of sugar does not feel out of kilter with the rest of the wine because it is balanced by the acidity. In the best off-dry wines, the sugar is naturally present in the grapes: the winemaker stops the fermentation before all the sugar has been turned into alcohol, as happens in dry wines.

"A range of styles, all with a little touch of sweetness."

WHITE WINE STYLES

5 RICH AND SWEET
Sauternes

Appearance Bright straw, gold, or amber.

Rich, sweet white wines are made from grapes with a far higher ratio of skins to juice than in dry white wines, which results in more pigment from the skins. The grapes are deliberately shrivelled – by leaving them in the sun before or after picking, by letting them freeze on the vine (to make ice wine) or, as with Sauternes, by "noble rot" when the fungus Botrytis cinerea *grows over ripe grapes on the vine.*

Aroma Intensely rich dried fruit, plus marmalade and honey.

The concentrated dried fruit aromas reflect the extremely ripe and/or raisined grapes.

Flavour Think crystallized and dried, not fresh fruit. Also toffee, marmalade, honey, and a mandarin-like zestiness. Very sweet.

In climates with a long ripening season – with a long, dry but not too warm autumn – the grapes can ripen but retain their acidity.

Texture Intensely rich and viscous, somewhere between dry white wine and honey. Long finish.

The high ratio of sugar in the grapes has been so concentrated by the shrivelling that the yeast cannot turn it all into alcohol.

This wine is made by the famous Sauternes producer Château de Climens

"Hedonistic – a dessert in itself."

Choosing Your Wine

Now that you have some idea of the range of white wine styles available, you can start looking for different wines in each category.

1 CRISP AND DRY Whites

Crisp and dry are the freshest style of whites. Light in body and subtle in aroma, they are refreshing on a summer's day.

Buying advice In general, look for young wines – drink them within a year or two of the vintage.
Food pairing Perfect for seafood.
Also try Names such as Soave, Muscadet, Chablis, Pinot Grigio, Aligoté, Verdicchio, Chasselas, and Picpoul de Pinet.

2 FRUITY AND DRY Whites

Similar to crisp and dry whites in terms of freshness, these aromatic wines have a more vibrant fruit flavour.

Buying advice Again, drink these young – within a year or two of the vintage.
Food pairing Fish, seafood; mild Asian food.
Also try Names such as Albariño, Sauvignon Blanc, Grüner Veltliner, dry Riesling, Jurançon, Gavi, Arneis, and Assyrtiko.

3 RICH AND DRY Whites

These full-bodied, full-flavoured wines, often from warmer climates, taste of very ripe fruit and have a creamy texture.

Buying advice Can age well – particularly the best examples from Australia and France.
Food pairing Rich fish dishes and white meat.

Also try Chardonnay from Burgundy's Côte d'Or, Australia, the USA, and South Africa; Marsanne; Sémillon; Chenin Blanc; white Rioja.

4 GENTLY SWEET Whites

This category features wines of many flavour profiles, united by a slightly sweet style balanced with acidity.

Buying advice Look at the back label for advice on sweetness. Key words include *demi-sec* (France) and *Kabinett* or *Spätlese* (Germany).
Food pairing The touch of sweetness works brilliantly with spicy food, helping to absorb the heat of chilli or pepper.
Also try Pinot Gris, Gewürztraminer, Riesling, and many Chenin Blancs can be found in an off-dry style; a lot of Vinho Verde is light and just off-dry and has a slight fizz, as does Moscato d'Asti.

5 RICH AND SWEET Whites

Made from grapes with a high concentration of sugar, these wines are sweet, rich, golden, and viscous.

Buying advice The very best can last for decades, but can be expensive.
Food pairing Rich and sweet wines work very well with desserts, but they also match up with hard and blue cheese and rich liver pâté.
Also try Sweet wines from Monbazillac and Jurançon in France; Tokaji from Hungary; German and Austrian TBA Riesling.

Explore

Red Wine Styles

As with white wine, red wines come in an enormous
variety of different styles. Over the course of this taste test
we'll be looking at five red styles that go all the way from
from the extremely light to the very powerful.

Weight variation

As we have seen in the section on understanding the basic differences between wine (pp.30–37), red wines will always feel weightier than white wines. This is because they have spent more time in contact with the grape skins during winemaking and those skins contain more of the natural chemical compounds known as tannins. However, as you begin to explore the world of red wine, you will start to see that different red wines will have varying weights.

The styles

The first set of wines we'll be looking at in this section are light, elegant reds, which can be almost like a rosé wine in colour. They may be light in texture, but in their own way these wines can still have very strong personalities. Closely related to the light, elegant reds are wines that are fresh and fruity. Characterized by bright fruit aromas and a certain drinkable juiciness, they are designed predominantly for refreshment – in fact, in France they are called *vins de soif* (literally "wines of thirst"). These refreshing red wines can be enjoyed slightly chilled, usually during warm, summer months. Smooth fruity reds have a bit more density, but they are also characterized by their bright fruit flavours leaping out of the glass, along with a soft and rounded texture. Last, but by no means least, are the two "heaviest" styles, both of which come into their own during the cold winter months. Rich and powerful reds are dark and dense in colour and flavour. Sweet and fortified reds are the wine world's digestifs – the perfect end to a meal.

Saint Émilion *Haut Gravet Grand Cru is a dark, full-bodied red with plenty of tannin.*

Tasting Session

1 LIGHT AND ELEGANT
Spätburgunder
Made from the Pinot Noir grape
variety, these German red wines
are light in colour and texture,
but have complex red fruit flavours
and a lovely supple texture.

Look for Georg Breuer
Spätburgunder; Franz Künstler
Spätburgunder Tradition

Serve at
14°C (57°F)

Grape Variety
*Spätburgunder
(aka Pinot Noir)*

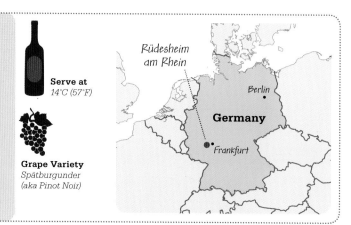

2 FRESH AND FRUITY
Beaujolais
The Gamay grape makes for
succulent, vivacious berry-scented
wines with a light but lively feel,
from the Beaujolais region to the
south of Burgundy in France.

Look for Henry Fessy Côte de
Brouilly; Château de Pizay
Beaujolais

Serve at
*12–14°C
(54–57°F)*

Grape Variety
Gamay

3 SMOOTH AND FRUITY
Chilean Merlot
Full-flavoured ripe fruit and soft
tannins are the hallmark of the
affordable red wines made in
Chile's warm, sunny Central Valley.

Look for Viña Casablanca Cefiro
Reserva Merlot; Concha y Toro
Casillero del Diablo Merlot

Serve at
14°C (55°F)

Grape Variety
Merlot

4 RICH AND POWERFUL
Californian Syrah blend

Dark in colour, the complex red wines of California are also full of dark fruit and tannin, filling the mouth with flavour.

Look for Tablas Creek Côtes de Tablas; Fess Parker Syrah

Serve at
13°C (55°F)

Grape Varieties
Syrah, Grenache, Mourvèdre

California, USA

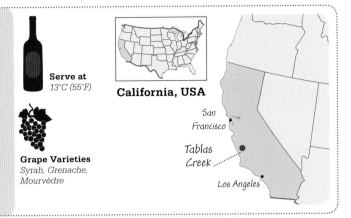

San Francisco

Tablas Creek

Los Angeles

5 SWEET AND FORTIFIED
Port

Made by adding grape spirit to red wine in Portugal's Douro Valley, Port is lusciously rich and sweet but never cloying.

Look for Graham's Crusted Port; Taylor's Late Bottled Vintage Port

Serve at
18°C (64°F)

Grape Varieties
Touriga Nacional, Touriga Francesa, Tinta Roriz, Tinta Baroca, Tinta Cão

Douro Valley

Porto

Lisbon

Portugal

Vineyards of the Chianti wineries,
which produce smooth, fruity reds, blanket the Tuscan hills between Florence and Siena.

1 LIGHT AND ELEGANT
Spätburgunder

 Appearance Pale cherry-red.

If a wine is light-coloured it will often (but not always) be light in texture, too. This wine has been made from the thin-skinned Pinot Noir grape variety.

 Aroma Gently aromatic. Red fruit – strawberries, raspberries – and a subtle earthy streak.

This style of red wine usually has fruit flavours towards the "red" end of the spectrum. The Pinot Noir variety often has a savoury or earthy edge.

 Flavour Succulent red fruit, a touch of citrus and cranberry.

The more delicate red wines are usually made in cooler climates where plenty of acidity is retained in the grapes at harvest, giving the fruit character a refreshing lift.

 Texture Dry but not astringent or drying. Light and silky.

Light elegant reds are made from grapes that are naturally lower in tannin than more powerful styles; their weight on the tongue has less impact, but rewards attention.

GEORG BREUER

(GB)

SPÄTBURGUNDER
Rouge

2006

RHEINGAU

Spätburgunder is the German word for the Pinot Noir grape variety

"Perfumed and delicate with a silky feel."

2 FRESH AND FRUITY
Beaujolais

 Appearance Vividly bright ruby-red to purple.

This is the colour of a youthful wine. Fresh fruity reds are best drunk young (within a year or two of the vintage) before they lose their vibrant colour and flavours.

 Aroma Lively, just-picked raspberry and blackberry, maybe with a floral (violet) edge.

Many fresh fruity reds are made using a technique called carbonic maceration which preserves the vibrant fruit aromas and flavours but can bring banana and bubblegum flavours in unskilled hands.

 Flavour More of that really vibrant fruit and fresh acidity.

Fresh fruity wines are generally made without being aged in new oak barrels that add the toasty flavours in rich dry whites.

 Texture Dry, light, and juicy with very little tannin.

The grapes used for fresh fruity reds usually have thin skins and big berries, making them juicy and low in tannin (which comes from skins and pips). They should be served slightly cooler than other reds.

The best Beaujolais have the village's name on the label

"Crunchy, succulent, berry fruit."

3 SMOOTH AND FRUITY
Chilean Merlot

Appearance Dark, deep cherry-red.

Smooth fruity reds are generally made with thicker-skinned grape varieties, with the juice given more contact with the skins, than the previous two styles.

Aroma Ripe black fruit such as black cherry, blackcurrant, and plum.

Smooth fruity reds generally come from warmer climates (such as Chile's benign Central Valley) than the lighter reds, and the fruit takes on a riper, darker cast.

Flavour Fleshy plum and cherry fruit. A subtle touch of coffee or vanilla flavour.

The ripe fruit of this style is often rounded off by ageing it in oak barrels, imparting those sweet coffee and vanilla flavours.

Texture Medium-bodied and fleshy. Feels denser than the lighter wines, but smooth.

Smooth fruity reds have more tannin and alcohol than lighter styles, but these characteristics are not to the foreground thanks to the lushly ripe fruit.

Wines labelled with a grape variety may include up to 25% of other varieties

"Fleshy and soft, with ripe fruit to the fore."

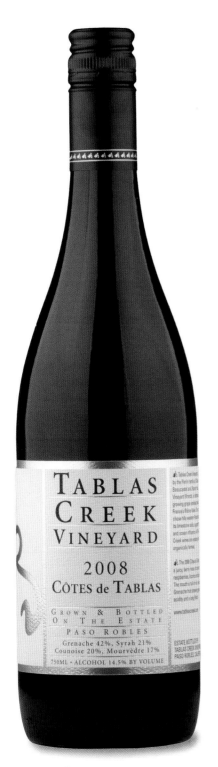

4 RICH AND POWERFUL
Californian Syrah blend

 Appearance Dense, dark, almost opaque purple.

Rich powerful reds are made from grapes with thick skins and small berries, bringing a much darker, deeper colour.

 Aroma Dark fruit, coffee, chocolate, maybe some vanilla or smokiness.

As with all wines, aromas vary depending on the grape varieties used and the location they are grown in, but rich and powerful reds respond well to ageing in new oak barrels, bringing complex aromas.

 Flavour Deep and concentrated dark fruit and dried fruit with coffee, chocolate, and vanilla.

Rich and powerful reds are usually produced in warmer climates where the thick skins have plenty of sun and warmth to ripen.

 Texture Dense and dry. Feels heavy and big in the mouth.

The grapes for this style have more sugar and tannin, with more alcohol and tannin found in the finished wines.

"Concentrated in flavour, and weighty in texture, these are the wine world's powerhouses."

5 SWEET AND FORTIFIED
Port

 Appearance Opaque purple fading to ruby or brick at the rim.

Port winemakers aim to get as much colour from their grapes as possible before they are fermented. Traditionally they do this by treading on them in stone troughs.

 Aroma Intense dried fruit, dark fruit jam or compote, spice, and chocolate.

Port grapes are grown in the very warm Douro Valley in Portual, where the long, hot summer lets them develop rich fruit flavours.

 Flavour As with the nose, dense dried and black fruit, spice, and chocolate. Sweet, intense.

Sweet red wines taste sweet because there is more sugar in the wine. In the case of Port, the winemaker adds spirit to stop the fermentation before all the sugar has been turned to alcohol, making a fortified wine.

 Texture Very smooth but weighty and firm.

Port has plenty of tannins from the thick skins, but it usually feels smooth after careful ageing in large oak barrels. Alcohol content is higher than other wines – 20%.

Crusted is a style of Port named after the harmless sediment or "crust" formed in the bottle

"Lusciously smooth but powerful sweet red wines."

Choosing Your Wine

Try your favourite red style with a suggested food pairing, and explore different examples of the other styles to see if your preferences alter.

1 LIGHT AND ELEGANT Reds

Pale but interesting, light elegant reds are usually made in cooler climates and have a subtle but complex flavour profile.

Buying advice Many examples of this style can age well – seek advice from your wine merchant.
Food pairing White meat and meatier fish dishes.
Also try Seek out examples of Pinot Noir from Burgundy, New Zealand, and Oregon; Cabernet Franc from the Loire Valley.

2 FRESH AND FRUITY Reds

Vibrantly fruity with low tannins, these succulent reds with plenty of acidity are great served chilled on a summer's day.

Buying advice This style of wine is best drunk young – before the vibrant fruit dies away.
Food pairing Poultry, gently cured cold meats, and meaty fish.
Also try Dolcetto and Valpolicella from northern Italy; Tarrango from Australia.

3 SMOOTH AND FRUITY Reds

Fleshy, ripe and rounded in the mouth, and medium-bodied, smooth fruity reds are easy to drink and generous in flavour.

Buying advice A broad category of wines that covers a wide range of prices – the best of this style ages beautifully.
Food pairing Pasta, pizza, pork, light meats.

Also try Merlot from Bordeaux, California, and Washington State; Rioja; Chianti; Montepulciano d'Abruzzo.

4 RICH AND POWERFUL Reds

The heavyweights of the wine world, these powerful long-lived wines are dense in colour and flavour, with deep black fruit and lots of tannin and alcohol.

Buying advice Wines from this category may need a few years for the flavours to mellow and harmonize – five years or more after the vintage.
Food pairing Roasted or grilled red meat; rich meat stews.
Also try Cabernet Sauvignon from Bordeaux and California; Barolo; Syrah from the Rhône Valley; Shiraz from Australia.

5 SWEET AND FORTIFIED Reds

Powerful but smooth, sweet and fortified reds are high in alcohol, making them rich and warming.

Buying advice Vintage Port and other sweet fortified wines can age for decades. Cheaper styles are ready for drinking now.
Food pairing Chocolate and chocolate puddings; hard cheeses.
Also try Port-style wines from Australia, South Africa, and the USA; Banyuls and Maury from southern France; Mavrodaphne Patras from Greece.

Explore

Rosé Wine Styles

Increasingly popular around the world, and no longer regarded as the poor relation of white and red, rosé gets its name from the French word for pink, but this style can come in a number of shades.

Not just a glass of pink

It's all too easy to find restaurants and bars that simply offer drinkers a glass of unspecified rosé, as if the name alone conveys all the information anyone might need to know about that particular wine's style. However, even though stylistic diversity isn't as wide with rosé as it is with red and white wines, not all pink wines are alike (or even very pink).

There are, in essence, three principal styles of rosé. The first is very pale in colour, and is dry and fresh; you might well think it is a dry white wine if you were unable to see its colour. The second style is also dry, but it is bolder in colour and flavour, and could almost be confused with a very light red wine. The third is also quite pale in colour, but will usually taste of sweet, almost candied fruit.

Santa Rita is *an example of a medium-bodied and dry rosé.*

Tasting Session

1 CRISP AND LIGHT
Rosé de Provence

A very pale rosé from the south of France with subtle red fruit and citrusy freshness.

Look for Clos Ste-Magdeleine Cassis Rosé; MIP (Made in Provence); Côtes de Provence Rosé

Serve at
8°C (46°F)

Grape Varieties
Grenache, Cinsault, Mourvèdre

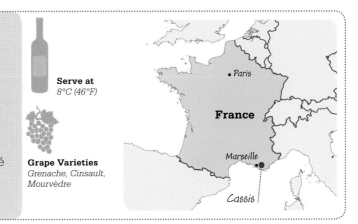

2 MEDIUM-BODIED AND DRY
Spanish Rosado

Rosé (also known locally as Rosado) is produced throughout Spain and it usually offers bold berry flavours.

Look for Marqués de Cáceres Rioja Rosado; various Torres Rosados

Serve at
8°C (46°F)

Grape Varieties
Garnacha, Cariñena

---

3 MEDIUM SWEET
Californian White Zinfandel

Not a white wine, but a medium-sweet, bright pink wine made from the Californian red grape variety, Zinfandel.

Look for Gallo Family Vineyards White Zinfandel; Sutter Home White Zinfandel

Serve at
6°C (43°F)

Grape Variety
Zinfandel

California, USA

1 CRISP AND LIGHT
Rosé de Provence

Clos Ste-Magdeleine is a top rosé producer in the Cassis area of Provence

Appearance Pale salmon or onion-skin.

Provençal rosés are made from the same red grape varieties as the region's darkly coloured red wines, but the juice is separated from the skins a few hours after they have been crushed.

Aroma Very subtle notes of red and white berries and blossom.

There's always a lightness and delicacy in Provençal rosés; only the subtle berry notes really distinguish them from a white wine.

Flavour Crisp citrus – pink grapefruit – with a touch of cranberry and strawberry.

This style of wine is fermented at cold temperatures in neutral stainless steel – just like a white wine – to preserve its delicate fruit flavours. For the same reason, the grapes are usually harvested in the cooler night-time or early morning.

Texture Light and elegant. Very refreshing and clean finish.

In Provence, where red grapes fare best in the warm climate, rosés fulfil the role of white wines in summer, where they are drunk with fish and lighter foods.

"Elegant, delicate, and zingily fresh and crisp."

2 MEDIUM-BODIED AND DRY
Spanish Rosado

 Appearance Bold, vibrant cherry-pink.

Spanish rosados are usually made with a greater amount of contact between the skin and juice than is common in Provence.

 Aroma Ripe berries – strawberries, cherries. Maybe a dash of black pepper.

Many Spanish rosados are made from the Garnacha grape, of which these are characteristic aromas, even in red wines made from this same variety.

 Flavour Dry but alive with full-flavoured strawberries-and-cream and succulent cranberry-like acidity.

The classic Garnacha flavours combine well with salty foods such as almonds and chorizo.

 Texture Medium-bodied, but crisp and finishing clean.

There is sometimes a very subtle note of astringency in Spanish rosado, which stems from the small amount of tannin extracted from the skins.

The clear glass bottle helps show off the bright colour of the wine

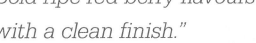

"Bold ripe red-berry flavours with a clean finish."

3 MEDIUM SWEET
Californian White Zinfandel

Appearance Very bright but very pale pink.

Not for nothing are Californian rosés known as "blush" wines. They have just a hint of colour from short skin-contact.

Aroma Not especially intense notes of watermelon, peach, and boiled strawberry-flavoured sweets.

White Zinfandel is generally made from vineyards with large crops, meaning the grape bunches are not hugely concentrated with flavour.

Flavour Sweet – a little like candy floss or a fruit-flavoured soft-drink.

Winemakers intentionally finish the fermentation before all the sugar has turned into alcohol, leaving a little sugar in the finished wine.

Texture Light and a little cloying unless served very cold.

The Zinfandel grape is not high in acidity, so the sugar is very noticeable. This impression is reduced at lower serving temperatures.

The Gallo family is one of America's largest wine producers

"Candy floss and strawberry sweets."

Choosing Your Wine

The quintessential summer wine, rosé has taken off in the past few years as people have learned to appreciate its subtle charms all year round, and many winemakers all over the world have added a rosé to their repertoire.

1 CRISP AND LIGHT **Rosés**

Light and refreshingly dry with citrus and delicate red fruits, Provençal rosés are great for drinking with a meal.

Buying advice Look for appellations such as Cassis, Côtes de Provence, Coteaux d'Aix-en-Provence, and Coteaux Varois.

Food pairing Great with that Provençal *salade Niçoise* and other fish and seafood.

Also try Rosés made from Pinot Noir around the world, particulary in Sancerre in the Loire Valley, France.

2 MEDIUM-BODIED AND DRY **Rosés**

Vivid colour and ripe berry fruit are in abundance in the more robust Spanish style of rosé, frequently made from the Garnacha grape variety.

Buying advice Look to Navarra and Rioja for the best quality Spanish rosados.

Food pairing Fish, grilled chicken; paella and risotto; charcuterie.

Also try Dry rosés from Australia, Argentina, Chile, and Tavel and Lirac in France's Rhône Valley.

3 MEDIUM SWEET **Rosés**

Sweet and sugary but light in alcohol, White Zinfandel is a highly popular style with flavours of strawberry sweets and candy floss.

Buying advice There are no particular standout producers of this style – it's widely available and should always be quite affordable.

Food pairing Chilled, its sugar content makes a decent match for the chillies in lighter, mildly spicy Asian food.

Also try Other off-dry and sweet rosé styles such as Rosé d'Anjou from France's Loire Valley, or the Portuguese brand, Mateus Rosé.

__A glass of__ chilled rosé wine is an increasingly popular choice all year round.

2

Build on it

Now that you are familiar with wine's many different styles, it's time to start exploring its ingredients and regions. Learn about the flavours and textures of grape varieties such as Chardonnay and Cabernet Sauvignon, and see what makes the red wines of Bordeaux taste so different from those of California.

In this section, learn about:

White Grape Varieties
pp.66–77

Red Grape Varieties
pp.78–89

Classic European Whites
pp.90–101

Classic European Reds
pp.102–113

Classic New World Whites
pp.114–121

Classic New World Reds
pp.122–129

Sparkling Wines
pp.130–137

Explore

White Grape Varieties

The Vitis vinifera species of vine used in wine production has many thousands of varieties. Although there are exceptions, most white wines are made from vines producing white grape varieties – each of which bring their own flavours and characteristics to the wine. In this section you'll get to know six of the most widely used white grapes.

Top celebrities

They say that imitation is the sincerest form of flattery, in which case the winemakers of Burgundy and the Loire Valley in France should be blushing with pride. These are the spiritual homes, the originators when it comes to producing wines from the world's two most popular white wine grape varieties – Sauvignon Blanc (from the Loire Valley) and Chardonnay (from Burgundy).

Sauvignon Blanc makes dry, fruity aromatic wines full of verve and with a distinctive leafy green tang. Also used in the whites of Bordeaux, outside France it is most strongly associated with New Zealand, and, increasingly, South Africa and Chile. Chardonnay is pretty much ubiquitous in the wine world, and makes a full spectrum of dry wines from the crisp, flinty style of Chablis in Burgundy to the warm, generous, golden styles of California.

Catching up fast with this pair, is Pinot Grigio, which actually has quite dark skins, but in northern Italy is used to make a light, crisp white. In Alsace and New Zealand, where it goes by the name of Pinot Gris, it makes powerfully aromatic off-dry whites.

Rising stars

The other three grape varieties in this section have not quite achieved the same levels of international fame, although many examples of each can be found across the world. Versatile Riesling is known for its fine blade of acidity and its floral tones in wines both dry and sweet, and thrives in Germany, Austria, and France's Alsace region, as well as Australia, New Zealand, and parts of the USA. Chenin Blanc is the Loire Valley's other great white grape variety, but it also makes complex, rich wines in South Africa. And finally Gewürztraminer, which is most commonly found in Alsace, produces musky, heady, perfumed, highly distinctive wines.

As you taste these wines, you'll be looking for what's known as varietal character: the pure fruit flavours that are distinctive to specific grape varieties. Try to make a note of those characters – how do they differ in each wine?

Gewürztraminer grapes, *which are grown mainly in France, are used to make dry and sweet wines.*

Tasting Session

1 CHARDONNAY
Chile

Winemakers produce Chardonnay throughout Chile, generally in a richer style with lots of ripe fruit. The best quality comes from cooler sites, such as Casablanca or Leyda.

Look for Casa Lapostolle Cuvée Alexandre Chardonnay; Loma Larga Chardonnay

Serve at
*10–12°C
(50–54°F)*

Grape Variety
Chardonnay

Chile

Santiago

Cunaco

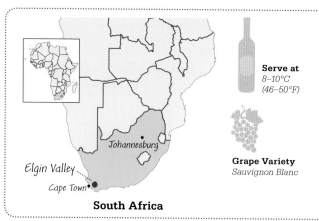

Johannesburg

Elgin Valley

Cape Town

South Africa

Serve at
*8–10°C
(46–50°F)*

Grape Variety
Sauvignon Blanc

2 SAUVIGNON BLANC
South Africa

South African winemakers have really taken to Sauvignon Blanc in the past couple of decades, making pure, crisp examples, particularly in cooler spots such as Elgin to the southeast of Cape Town.

Look for Iona Sauvignon Blanc; Tokara Sauvignon Blanc

---

3 RIESLING
Washington State, USA

Generally associated with cool northern Europe, Riesling has found a home in the near-desert conditions of the US Pacific Northwest, where it makes fruity, aromatic wines.

Look for Pacific Rim Wallula Vineyard Riesling; Chateau Ste Michelle Eroica Riesling

Serve at
*8–10°C
(46–50°F)*

Grape Variety
Riesling

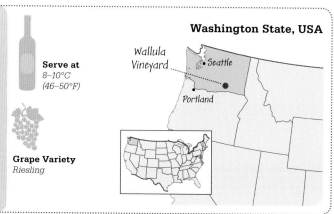

Washington State, USA

Wallula Vineyard

Seattle

Portland

4 CHENIN BLANC
Loire Valley, France

Chenin Blanc has many styles from dry to sweet, but always with a certain richness. We'll be looking at a classic dry style from the variety's homeland, the Loire Valley.

Look for Domaine Huet Le Haut Lieu Sec Vouvray; Domaine La Grange aux Belles Fragile Anjou

Serve at
*10–12°C
(50–54°F)*

Grape Variety
Chenin Blanc

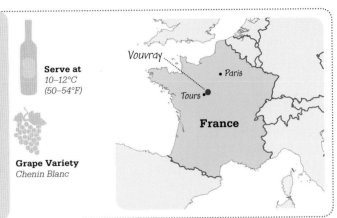

5 PINOT GRIGIO/GRIS
Northeast Italy

Many examples can be neutral to the point of bland, but the best Pinot Grigio from the far northern Italian regions of Friuli and the Alto Adige is gently aromatic.

Look for Livio Felluga Pinot Grigio Colli Orientali; Elena Walch Pinot Grigio, Alto Adige

Serve at
8°C (46°F)

Grape Variety
Pinot Grigio

6 GEWÜRZTRAMINER
Alsace, France

Love-it-or-hate-it Gewürztraminer is highly perfumed with musky floral scents. Made in dry, off-dry, and fully sweet styles, it reaches its finest expression in Alsace.

Look for Maison Paul Zinck Alsace Gewürztraminer; Hugel Alsace Gewürztraminer

Serve at
*10–12°C
(50–54°F)*

Grape Variety
Gewürztraminer

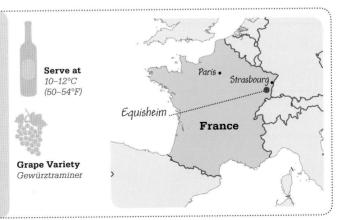

1 CHARDONNAY
Chile

Appearance Seductive bright yellow-gold.

Chardonnay grapes ripen from green to yellow gold. This Chardonnay is made in a region with a long, warm growing season, with the grapes harvested at full ripeness.

Aroma Ripe generous fruit: pineapple, banana, and melon. Some subtle toasty, nutty, and vanilla notes.

The ripeness of the grapes comes through in those richer fruit flavours. In cooler regions, where the grapes are not so ripe, such as Burgundy in France, Chardonnay's character tends more to citrus or orchard fruit.

Flavour Lots of ripe pineapple, banana, melon. Also creamy, buttery notes. Toasted nuts, vanilla, butterscotch.

The Chardonnay variety has a particular affinity with oak flavours and aromas (nutty, vanilla, toasty), and many Chardonnays are made with oak barrels.

Texture Rich, weighty in the mouth, with a creamy, buttery feeling, but a fresh finish.

Chardonnay is often made with malolactic fermentation, a process more usually associated with red wine that converts tart malic acid into softer lactic acid, giving a richer, buttery feel (see p.17).

Casablanca is one of Chile's best Chardonnay regions.

"Golden, rich, generous, and creamy."

Lapostolle

Cuvée
Alexandre

CHARDONNAY

ATALAYAS VINEYARD
CASABLANCA VALLEY

2 SAUVIGNON BLANC
South Africa

Appearance Bright pale straw with green tinges.

This colour is typical of Sauvignon Blanc made in stainless steel tanks rather than oak barrels.

Aroma Cut grass, asparagus, and gooseberry. Some citrus and pineapple. Intensely aromatic.

Sauvignon Blanc always has a verdant greenness to its aroma. In warmer climates, more tropical notes begin to emerge. South African styles generally combine both.

Flavour More of that intense juicy green fruit, underpinned by citrus, particularly grapefruit.

In some Sauvignon Blanc, the green flavours can take over, becoming more like tinned green pepper or asparagus – usually due to under-ripe grapes from over-vigorous vines. Many people enjoy those flavours, however, and producers have been known to add (illegally) factory-produced green-pepper flavours to their wines.

Texture Feels vibrant and fresh in the mouth; clean and crisp.

The best Sauvignon Blanc always comes from climates favourable to retaining acidity in the grapes: a warm climate with cooling sea breezes (like Elgin in South Africa), or with warm days and cool nights (as in much of Chile); or a mild climate such as the Loire Valley.

iona

ELGIN

SAUVIGNON BLANC

2009

SOUTH AFRICA

Sea-breezes make Elgin a great spot for Sauvignon Blanc.

"Vibrantly verdant, fresh, aromatic, dry white."

3 RIESLING
Washington State, USA

Appearance Bright yellow with silver tints.

The Riesling grape often produces a silver tint in young wines.

Aroma Gently aromatic. Flowers, orchard fruit – apples, pears, yellow plum – peaches, lime.

Riesling is a naturally aromatic grape, and it is never made with an oak influence. Winemakers use either stainless steel or large, old oak barrels that do not have the toasty flavours of new oak when they are making Riesling. Its aromas develop over time to include petrol and toast.

Flavour Zesty fruit dominates, with a fine blade of steel-like acidity. Many Rieslings exhibit a wet stone mineral finish.

The Riesling variety is naturally high in acidity, giving a distinctive cleansing tang. Depending on where it is grown, it takes on mineral, wet-stone characters – particularly on the slate soils of the Mosel in Germany (see p.96), but also, in this example, on the complex mix of soils in Washington State's Columbia Valley.

Texture Rieslings go from light and delicately sweet to fully sweet and unctuous, via light and dry.

Riesling is a grape that can develop complex flavours (physiological ripeness) even before it reaches full sugar ripeness. This means it can be made in a light style, with low alcohol (remember, the alcohol content of a wine is defined by the amount of sugar in the grapes) without sacrificing flavour. It is also often made with sugar left in the wine to balance out the pronounced acidity.

The Pacific Rim winery is a Riesling specialist

Pacific Rim

RIESLING

WALLULA VINEYARD
Columbia Valley

"Floral, delicate, and aromatic with a sharp blade of acidity."

4 CHENIN BLANC
Loire Valley, France

Top Chenin Blancs can age for decades

Appearance Bright straw-yellow turning to gold with age.

Chenin Blanc is a late-ripening grape that takes on a yellow colour as it ripens.

Aroma Hay, quince, baked apples, honey.

Chenin Blanc's richness of aroma intensifies with age, with fresh apple giving way to the distinctive honey and hay or damp straw.

Flavour Following the nose, rich and intense with a pleasingly sour tang.

If pleasing sourness sounds odd, think of the tartness of apples or quince jelly – it works when offset against the richness of the other flavours.

Texture Can be bone-dry, off-dry, or sweet, yet usually full-bodied. Tangy finish. Chalky.

Chenin Blanc's naturally high acidity works well in sweet wines, where the sugar is balanced by the freshness. In the dry Chenin Blancs of Savennières in the Loire Valley and South Africa, the balance of rich fruit and also those from a chalky toughness of texture is like no other white wine.

"Rich, full-bodied, distinctively honeyed with a sweet-sour tang, and a tough-and-tender texture."

LE HAUT-LIEU
SEC
2011

DOMAINE HUET
VOUVRAY
APPELLATION VOUVRAY CONTRÔLÉE
PRODUIT DE FRANCE · PRODUCT OF FRANCE

Grigio is Italian for grey – the grapes are dark but not black

Livio Felluga
Pinot Grigio
2006

The Friuli region makes high-quality Pinot Grigio

5 PINOT GRIGIO/GRIS
Northeast Italy

Appearance Very pale yellow with silver grey and occasionally a subtle pink tinge.

Pinot Grigio – Pinot Gris in France – has dark skins, but the juice is taken away from the skins straight after pressing the grapes.

Aroma Subtle, fresh notes of white flowers with delicate pear and apple.

This is the northeastern Italian style of Pinot Grigio. Alsace, Oregon, and New Zealand produce a more powerfully aromatic Pinot Gris, with peach, apricot, and spice.

Flavour Light, delicate flavours of pear and crisp lemony fruit.

Pinot Grigio can be light to the point of neutral, the result of "over-cropping" with too many bunches of grapes per vine. Pinot Gris has more spice and richer fruit.

Texture Very light-bodied; the best have a subtle fleshiness.

Picked early, Pinot Grigio grapes have plenty of acidity and less sugar – the more the sugar, the higher the alcohol, which gives weight to a wine's texture. Pinot Gris, in contrast, feels rich and fat in the mouth.

"Crisp and elegant as Italian Pinot Grigio; fat and spicy as French Pinot Gris."

6 GEWÜRZTRAMINER
Alsace, France

 Appearance   Pale amber-gold.

Gewürztraminer grapes have a delicate pink hue, rarely apparent in the finished wines.

 Aroma   Intensely aromatic and musky – lychees, rose-water, pot-pourri.

Why this intensity? Well, some grape varieties are naturally more aromatic than others. Compare a ripe Muscat grape with a Thompson Seedless the next time you're in a supermarket and note the difference.

 Flavour   More of those distinctively powerful floral notes, but with a touch of ginger, lemongrass, or galangal.

Gewürztraminer is grown all over the world in small quantities, but it rarely attains the spicy complexity of flavours found in Alsace.

 Texture   Fat, viscous, powerful. Clean finish.

With Gewürztraminer, the challenge for winemakers is to harvest at the right time before the acidity is so low and the sugar (and therefore alcohol) so high that the wines become unpleasantly oily and bitter.

It's not easy to tell the sweetness or dryness of a Gewürztraminer from the label

"Headily aromatic and easy to spot for its lychee-and-rose flavours."

Choosing Your Wine

The white grape varieties you've tasted in this section are just a small sample of the different grape varieties used around the world. There are many thousands more, and winemakers will often blend two or more grapes together, with each variety bringing a different personality, flavour, or texture to the wine.

A dry white wine *makes an excellent accompaniment to soft cheese.*

1 CHARDONNAY **Wines**

Grown all over the world, Chardonnay can be made as an unoaked fresh, crisp dry white, but responds well to oak, giving it a buttery, full-bodied, and golden character.

Buying advice Look to Chablis or wines labelled "unoaked" for the fresher style; spend a little more for the best examples of the richer style.
Food pairing Seafood for the fresh style; fish, white meat, and mushrooms for the richer style.
Also try In the rich dry style, try white wines from Rioja or the Rhône; for the fresher style try the Aligoté or Verdicchio grape varieties.

2 SAUVIGNON BLANC **Wines**

Pungently aromatic with characteristic notes of gooseberry and cut-grass, Sauvignon Blanc takes on tropical fruit flavours such as passion fruit and mango in warmer climates, but always with fresh, crisp acidity.

Buying advice Sauvignon Blanc is a wine that is best consumed when young – within 2 to 3 years of the vintage.
Food pairing Fish and seafood, goat's cheese, asparagus.
Also try Aromatic whites such as Albariño from Spain and Grüner Veltliner from Austria.

Piles of freshly picked white grapes *lie drying in the southern Spanish sunshine.*

3 RIESLING Wines

Riesling can be dry or sweet, but it is distinguished by its blade of acidity. Floral, peach, and orchard fruit flavours predominate when the wine is young; petrol and toasty aromas as it ages.
Buying advice Riesling can age beautifully – for decades in the best examples.
Food pairing Light fish dishes and mildly spicy Asian food.
Also try Floral aromatic whites made from the Muscat, Müller-Thurgau, or Sylvaner.

4 CHENIN BLANC Wines

This is another versatile grape variety that is made in all styles from dry to full sweet, with a pleasing contrast of richness, chalkiness and apple-like acidity, with characters of honey, quince, and hay.

Buying advice Check the sweetness levels. You may need to look at the back-label – in France Chenin moves from *sec* (dry) to *demi-sec* (sweeter), and *moelleux* (very sweet).

Food pairing Roast chicken for the drier styles; tarte Tatin with the richer, sweeter examples.
Also try Dry wines made from the Savagnin variety in Jura, France, Sémillon from Australia, Furmint from Hungary.

5 PINOT GRIGIO/GRIS Wines

Grey-skinned Pinot Grigio makes delicate, crisp dry whites with subtle pear and apple flavours and a hint of spice. When labelled as Pinot Gris, the same grape makes wines with apricot and spice.

Buying advice Remember the difference between Gris and Grigio – the former can keep for years, the latter is one for young drinking.
Food pairing Fish and seafood for Grigio; risotto, game and white meat for Gris.
Also try Other Italian white grape varieties such as Trebbiano (in Orvieto and Frascati) or Garganega (Soave) are made in a similar style to Pinot Grigio; Marsanne and Roussanne grapes make rich dry whites, similar in weight to Pinot Gris.

6 GEWÜRZTRAMINER Wines

Easy to spot from their scent of lychees and rosewater, Gewürztraminer makes opulently aromatic wines with a viscous palate in both dry and sweet styles.

Buying advice The best Gewürztraminer comes from Alsace in sites labelled "Grand Cru".
Food pairing Chinese and southeast Asian-style spiced cuisine.
Also try Torrontés and Muscat grapes have some of the aromatic qualities of Gewürztraminer in a lighter style; Viognier can also have a similar texture but with more peachy flavours.

Explore

Red Grape Varieties

Like their white equivalents, red grapes have travelled the world from their European homeland. Some red grapes are better travellers than others: here we'll look at six of the most frequently encountered, all of them with distinct personalities.

The big four

As with white wines, it is French varieties, or at least varieties that were first popularized in France, that dominate the production of quality red wines. These are led by what is sometimes known as the big four, each of which is strongly associated with a specific French region: Cabernet Sauvignon, Merlot, Pinot Noir, and Syrah.

Cabernet Sauvignon is a powerful, thick-skinned grape variety that shines in Bordeaux, creating strong, textured wines with a firm backbone of tannin and acidity, and flavours of cassis. Its global reach is wide, but it has had particular success in California, Chile, Argentina, Australia, and Italy's Tuscan coast.

Also associated with Bordeaux, and often a partner of Cabernet in blended wines both in the French region and around the world (known as "Bordeaux blends"), Merlot produces softer, fleshier reds with a dark plum, black cherry, and chocolate character.

Burgundy's contribution to red wine producers is Pinot Noir, which produces light, elegant, and racy reds, full of red fruits. While Burgundy is still the undisputed king of Pinot, it has had competition in recent years from Oregon, New Zealand, California, Australia, and Chile. Syrah is an important grape of the Rhône Valley, both on its own (producing sinewy, meaty reds with black pepper and blackberry flavours), and as part of a blend with juicy, jammy Grenache. It has been taken up with enthusiasm in Australia, where it is known as Shiraz, and where it makes dense, inky, sweetly black-fruited reds. It is also widely planted throughout Chile, South Africa, the USA, New Zealand, and the south of France.

The next two

Besides the big four is Grenache, known as Garnacha in Spain. It plays a supporting role in many of the wines of Rioja, alongside the most important Spanish red wine grape, Tempranillo, a versatile variety that is known variously as Tinta Fino, Tinto del País, Tinta del Toro, and, in Portugal, Tinta Roriz and Aragones. Despite its versatility, Tempranillo has not really caught on outside Iberia, with a handful of exceptions in Australia, Oregon, and Argentina.

Many red wines today feature the grape variety on the label, and they are good guide to the flavours you can expect in the bottle.

Cabernet Sauvignon *grapes are one of the most popular varieties, grown across the world.*

① ② ③

Tasting Session

1 CABERNET SAUVIGNON
Chile

Most Chilean winemakers produce a Cabernet Sauvignon, and they are frequently good value, with bright cassis fruit.

Look for Cono Sur Cabernet Sauvignon; Errázuríz Cabernet Sauvignon

Serve at
16°C (61°F)

Grape Variety
Cabernet Sauvignon

Chile

Santiago

Chimbarongo

2 MERLOT
Washington State, USA

The Pacific Northwest of the USA has become strongly identified with Merlot: it sits on the same degree of latitude as Bordeaux, although the climates in these two areas differ.

Look for Horse Heaven Hills Columbia Crest Merlot; l'Ecole 41 merlot

Washington State, USA

Paterson

Seattle

Portland

Serve at
16°C (61°F)

Grape Variety
Merlot

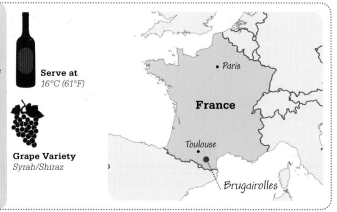

3 SYRAH/SHIRAZ
Languedoc, France

Syrah is widely planted throughout France's largest and most productive wine region, the Languedoc, where it makes powerful, spicy herb-scented examples.

Look for Domaine Gayda Syrah IGP Pays d'Oc; Domaine les Yeuses Les Épices Syrah IGP Pays d'Oc

Serve at
16°C (61°F)

Grape Variety
Syrah/Shiraz

Paris

France

Toulouse

Brugairolles

4 PINOT NOIR
Oregon, USA

In just a few decades, Washington State's neighbour in the Pacific Northwest of the USA, Oregon, has become a specialist in Pinot Noir, making wines in a plump but pure style in the Willamette Valley.

Look for Adelsheim Pinot Noir; Firesteed Pinot Noir

Serve at
14°C (57°F)

Grape Variety
Pinot Noir

Oregon, USA

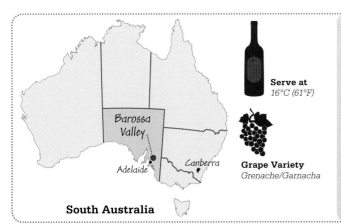

South Australia

Serve at
16°C (61°F)

Grape Variety
Grenache/Garnacha

5 GRENACHE/GARNACHA
South Australia

Grenache is often blended with Shiraz, but on its own it produces a bright and juicy, soft red with lots of red fruit and a touch of spice.

Look for Peter Lehmann Back to Back Grenache, Barossa Valley; d'Arenberg The Custodian Grenache, Barossa Valley

---

6 TEMPRANILLO
La Mancha, Spain

Tempranillo is most associated with the Rioja region of northeast Spain (see p.111), but it is produced across the country, and is famous for its soft strawberry flavours.

Look for Marqués de Calatrava Tempranillo, La Mancha; Ochoa Crianza Tempranillo

Serve at
16°C (61°F)

Grape Variety
Tempranillo

Spain

1 CABERNET SAUVIGNON
Chile

 Appearance Vibrant dark purple.

A thick-skinned grape, the Cabernet Sauvignon produces darkly coloured wines.

 Aroma Powerfully fruity: lots of ripe blackcurrant with maybe a slight minty touch.

Blackcurrant is the distinctive fruit flavour of Cabernet Sauvignon. The wines often have a slight green touch, which can be attractively minty (particularly in Chile) or eucalyptus (Australia's Coonawarra region), but can also veer towards green pepper and tomato stalk when the grapes aren't fully ripe.

 Flavour Bright flavours of blackcurrant, sometimes a touch of pencil lead and cedar wood.

Cabernet Sauvignon is frequently aged in oak barrels, a process which brings out those cedar-wood and pencil-lead flavours. As it ages, good Cabernet Sauvignon takes on even more of those savoury flavours such as cigar-box and tobacco, and even a certain meatiness.

 Texture Dry, quite chunky and chewy – almost angular – but with freshness on the finish.

Small berries and thick skins give young Cabernet its distinctive "structure": a combination of firm tannins and acidity which softens beautifully over time (five years to several decades), particularly in Bordeaux (see p.107).

Cono Sur

Wine of Chile
2010

Adolfo Hurtado, Winemaker

Cabernet Sauvignon

"Powerful and angular in structure with blackcurrant flavours."

The bicycle symbolizes Cono Sur's commitment to the environment

2 MERLOT
Washington State, USA

 Appearance Very dark red-purple.

Merlot has much thinner skins and larger berries than Cabernet Sauvignon, giving a red hue to its wines.

 Aroma Ripe plums, black cherries, and fruits of the forest. A touch of chocolate, coffee, vanilla, or fruitcake.

Early-ripening and ready to harvest before autumn rains threaten, Merlot is a popular grape but quite hard to grow: those thin skins are prone to rot and insects. When growers get it right, it offers gorgeous fruit.

 Flavour More of those ripe, fleshy almost sweet-plum and fruits-of-the-forest flavours.

Widely grown, Merlot wines are among the most variable in quality, and overcropping, with too much fruit per vine, lowers the concentration of flavour. The best examples, though, achieve a great intensity of soft fruit.

 Texture Ample, fleshy, and seductive with soft tannins.

Merlot is often planted alongside Cabernet Sauvignon: Merlot's texture is much softer, smoother, and less angular, making it a fine blending partner in Bordeaux and elsewhere.

"Soft and generous with fleshy plum and fruits of the forest."

83

3 SYRAH/SHIRAZ
Languedoc, France

 Appearance Dark, almost inky black-purple.

Thick skins full of pigment give Syrah wines their dark colour.

 Aroma Blackberry, black pepper, herbs, cinnamon, vanilla.

As with Pinot Grigio/Gris in our tasting of white grape varieties (p.74), Syrah and Shiraz share the same grape variety, but they represent quite different wine styles. Syrah is brighter, more pepper-spicy and savoury; Shiraz will generally have much richer, sweet-fruited aromas.

 Flavour Intense, following the nose in character, but also some savoury flavours of tar, leather, bacon fat, herbs. Chocolate.

Once again, much depends on whether the wine is made as Syrah or Shiraz. For the Syrah, expect more tarry, black-pepper qualities; for a Shiraz, expect sweeter fruit, shading to chocolate.

 Texture From slippery and lively to super-smooth, almost viscous.

Syrah, which is generally produced in cooler (though not cool) climates than Shiraz, has a slippery lighter-feeling texture thanks to a higher acidity remaining in the grapes; Shiraz, particularly in the very warm Australian region of Barossa, has much riper grapes with more sugar and therefore alcohol, but lower acidity, giving a much denser mouth-filling texture.

The Gayda estate incorporates the traditional cross of the Languedoc region in its logo.

"*A grape of two halves – supple, black-pepper spicy Syrah and smooth, richly fruited Shiraz.*"

4 PINOT NOIR
Oregon, USA

Appearance Bright ruby-red with a lighter ruby rim.

Pinot Noir is a thin-skinned grape producing lighter-coloured wines.

Aroma Red fruits – strawberry, cherry, raspberry. Maybe some floral and earthy notes, like a forest floor.

Pinot Noir flourishes in good vintages in cooler climates. Its thin skins need to ripen gently and slowly with lots of sun but without intense heat. Too much heat quickly brings jammy flavours; too little sun and the wines become unpleasantly sour, tart, and thin.

Flavour More of that red-fruits character – the fruit feels fresh, delicate, with an earthy undertone.

Pinot Noir is a tricky grape to work with in the winery. Too much contact between the grape skins and the juice, and the flavours lose their delicacy; too much new oak and they are obscured by toasty flavours.

Texture Light but insistent, silky, refreshing.

The best Pinot Noir never feels powerful and strong like Cabernet Sauvignon or Shiraz, but it has a silky touch that is unlike anything else – acidity is high, the tannins are light and graceful, and the alcohol is low.

Adelsheim takes its name from the company founders David and Ginny Adelsheim

The Willamette Valley is known for its high-quality Pinot Noir

"Elegant, perfumed, and silky light reds with a subtle power."

5 GRENACHE/GARNACHA
South Australia

Appearance Bright ruby-red, sometimes with an orange hue.

The thin skins of the Grenache grape (known as Garnacha in Spain) are low in pigment.

Aroma Ripe red fruits, occasionally shading into strawberry or raspberry jam. In some examples, complex notes of white pepper and wild herbs.

Grenache is late to ripen and needs plenty of sun and warmth. The most intense versions are made from low-yielding (low fruit per vine), old (several decades) vines.

Flavour Sweet ripe red fruit – berries, herbs, white pepper.

Generous sweet fruit and soft tannins make Grenache a fine counterpart to wines with darker fruit and stronger, firmer tannins.

Texture Rich, soft, juicy, and fleshy but powerful.

Grenache grapes accumulate lots of sugar by the time they reach full flavour ripeness, which means they have plenty of alcohol in the finished wine – generally above 14%.

The Back to Back brand is produced by the Peter Lehmann winery

"Sun-filled, sweetly red-fruited, and powerful."

6 TEMPRANILLO
La Mancha, Spain

Appearance Bright ruby-red with garnet tinges.

Tempranillo is a fairly thin-skinned grape. Ageing for long periods in oak barrels gives a garnet, brick-like tinge to the wine.

Aroma Strawberry, coconut, vanilla, and savoury flavours of leather and game.

The oak influence again – largely the result of traditional Spanish winemaking practices, with long ageing in American oak for that vanilla and coconut flavour.

Flavour More of that softly-scented strawberry. Savoury, gamey, and leathery aromas coming through more on the palate. Notes of tobacco and spice.

The mellow savouriness increases with age. The best Tempranillos from Spain's northwestern regions of Rioja, Ribera del Duero, and Toro can age for several decades.

Texture Medium-bodied with a mellow softness.

This is classic Tempranillo. However, some modern Spanish winemakers have started to make Tempranillo with a darker, more intense fruit character and more tannin.

This Tempranillo wine comes from the La Mancha region

"Mellow, soft, strawberry and coconut with savoury edges."

Choosing Your Wine

As with white grapes, there are thousands of different red grapes. The varieties we have explored in this section each add their own unique stamp of both taste and texture to the wines they produce. Depending on where they are made in the world, the grapes can produce markedly different flavours, but there will always be a family resemblance.

Red wines *get their colour and most of their particular flavour from the skin of the grape.*

2 MERLOT **Wines**

Frequently used as a partner to Cabernet Sauvignon (see above) in Bordeaux-style blends, Merlot makes fleshier, softer wines with dark plum, black cherry, and chocolate flavours and a smooth texture.

Buying advice Bordeaux regions Pomerol and St-Émilion provide the world's greatest Merlot wines.
Food pairing Roasted meat such as lamb, duck, or beef.
Also try Malbec from Argentina or Carménère from Chile.

1 CABERNET SAUVIGNON **Wines**

A well-travelled grape variety providing powerful, chewy-textured wines with flavours of blackcurrant, pencil-lead, and cedar wood, Cabernet Sauvignon is often found in partnership with Merlot.

Buying advice Chile produces good-value versions. Look to Bordeaux and California's Napa Valley for the greatest bottles.
Food pairing Roasted red meat and dark game.
Also try Italian Nebbiolo or Tannat from Madiran in southwest France or Uruguay.

3 SYRAH/SHIRAZ **Wines**

This single grape can make two distinct styles. The first, Syrah, tends towards black pepper and supple texture; Shiraz is denser, smoother with sweet black fruit.

Buying advice Look to France's northern Rhône valley and Languedoc regions and New Zealand for Syrah; Australia and South Africa for Shiraz.
Food pairing Rich meaty stews and red meat.
Also try Aglianico from southern Italy; Touriga Nacional from Portugal.

The Carménère grape *originated in France, but it is now predominantly grown in Chile.*

4 PINOT NOIR
Wines

This grape variety prefers a cooler climate where it makes light elegant reds with uniquely light, silky tannins, fresh acidity, and red fruit and earthy characters.

Buying advice Good Pinot is rarely cheap. Be prepared to spend to find decent examples, and spend very big for the best.

Food pairing Light game meat and even some meatier fish (salmon, tuna).

Also try Elegant aromatic reds such as Cabernet Franc from the Loire Valley in France; Mencía from Galicia in northwest Spain; Zweigelt from Austria.

5 GRENACHE/GARNACHA
Wines

Often a partner in blends, the hardy Grenache thrives in warm climates producing sun-filled, sweetly red-fruited wines seasoned with white pepper and herbs that are juicy in character and frequently high in alcohol.

Buying advice It won't tell you on the label, but Grenache is the senior partner in the famous Rhône Valley wines of Châteauneuf-du-Pape and Gigondas, and top Spanish red Priorat.

Food pairing Rich meaty stews and sausages.

Also try Compare and contrast with the denser wines made in similar climates from the Mourvèdre grape variety in Australia (South Australia and New South Wales), Provence (Bandol region), and Spain (Jumilla region). This grape is also known as Monastrell and Mataro.

6 TEMPRANILLO
Wines

Tempranillo is the most important Spanish red grape variety, and also important in Portugal's Douro Valley, but it is rarely seen elsewhere. Tempranillo is often aged for a long time in oak barrels yielding a wine with soft strawberry, coconut, and savoury flavours.

Buying advice Rioja is the king of Tempranillo. Look to Ribera del Duero and Toro for more powerful darker-fruited styles; La Mancha can offer good value examples.

Food pairing Braised or roasted pork and lamb.

Also try Medium-bodied, savoury wines such as Sangiovese from Tuscany's Chianti region or Xinomavro from Greece.

Explore

Classic European Whites

The great white wines of Europe are benchmarks for the
rest of the wine world and are produced all over the
continent. In this section you'll learn about six classic,
widely available styles that have stood the test of time.

White wine tour

We're now getting to the part where
learning about wine gets really interesting,
what wine marketing types call
"regionality" and what the more poetic
might like to think of as travelling the world,
bottle by bottle. For winemakers, the region
where the wine is made is just as important
as the grape variety used to make it. In fact,
many classic European wine regions don't
even mention the grape variety anywhere
on the label. Winemakers believe that good
wine is all about transmitting a distinctive
sense of place or region – that if you drink,
say, a glass of Chardonnay made in Chablis
right in the northern reaches of Burgundy,
France (a region that only makes
Chardonnay), it will not taste like a
Chardonnay produced anywhere else.

Local laws

The emphasis on keeping regional styles
distinct is reflected in European wine laws.
European winemakers who wish to make
wine that features a region on the label have
to obey certain laws that are imposed to
protect local practices. How strict those
rules are vary from region to region, but they
will usually cover the type of grape varieties
that are permitted, the maximum amount
of grapes that can be harvested per hectare
of vineyard land, and the amount of time
the wine has to spend ageing before it is
released. In wine shops and on restaurant
wine lists, these protected areas all across
Europe are generally referred to by the
French term *appellation*.

Region by region

In this tasting we're going to take a tour of
some of Europe's most celebrated white
wine regions, each with its own distinctive
taste and style. Each of these regions uses a
different grape variety – which of course has
an important influence on their flavours.
But in this taste test we will also start to
learn about the unique interplay between
land, tradition, and climate that makes each
regional style distinct.

Vineyards in Sancerre in the eastern Loire Valley,
one of the great French white wine-growing regions.

Tasting Session

1 CHABLIS
Burgundy, France

Chardonnay is the white grape of Burgundy, France, and in the area around the town of Chablis it produces bone-dry whites known for their steely, mineral character.

Look for Domaine William Fèvre Chablis or Domaine Daniel Dampt Chablis

Serve at
8–10°C
(46–50°F)

Grape Variety
Chardonnay

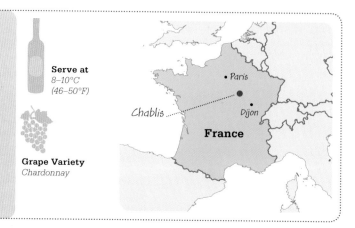

2 SANCERRE
Loire Valley, France

An appellation in the Loire Valley, Sancerre specializes in a single grape variety, Sauvignon Blanc, making white wines with grassy, gooseberry, and flinty flavours.

Look for Domaine Naudet Sancerre, Domaine Henri Bourgeois Sancerre

Serve at
8–10°C
(46–50°F)

Grape Variety
Sauvignon Blanc

3 RIESLING
Mosel, Germany

We will be looking at the classically light (7–9% alcohol) and elegant off-dry styles produced along the banks of the Mosel River.

Look for Top producer Weingut Max Ferd Richter Graacher Himmelreich Rieseling Kabinett; St Urbans-hof Riesling QbA

Serve at
8–10°C
(46–50°F)

Grape Variety
Riesling

4 ALBARIÑO
Rías Baixas, Spain

The Galician region of Rías Baixas in the northwest has a wetter, cooler climate than the rest of Spain that is perfectly suited to the richly aromatic Albariño grape.

Look for Castrocelta or Martin Códax Albariños are excellent alternatives

Serve at
8–10°C (46–50°F)

Grape Variety
Albariño

5 GRÜNER VELTLINER
Austria

The distinctive Grüner Veltliner grape is Austria's international calling-card; the best examples come from the eastern regions of Kamptal, Kremstal, and Wachau.

Look for Loimer Grüner Veltliner, Kamptal; Domäne Wachau Terraces

Serve at
12°C (54°F)

Grape Variety
Grüner Veltliner

6 SOAVE
Italy

A traditional favourite in Italian restaurants around the world, Soave can be bland, but the better stuff, produced in the Soave Classico area, has a light but graceful, almond-and-herbal charm.

Look for Inama Soave Classico; Pieropan Soave Classico

Serve at
8–10°C (46–50°F)

Grape Varieties
Garganega, Trebbiano, Chardonnay

1 CHABLIS
Burgundy, France

Appearance Bright, clear, pale-gold colour with a green tint.

Pale and green suggests a young wine from a cooler area – Chablis is in one of France's most northerly wine-growing regions.

Aroma A gentle mix of lemon, green apple, and white flowers with a subtle flinty edge like striking the wheel in a cigarette lighter.

Good Chablis whispers rather than shouts, avoiding the toast-and-vanilla aromas of other Chardonnays – in the more southerly parts of Burgundy and the rest of the world – that have been aged in new oak barrels.

Flavour Bone-dry with very fresh, almost sour green apple and lemon, plus more of that flintiness and minerality (think wet stones or a very tasty mineral water).

Chablis' famed minerality is generally attributed to its fossil and limestone soils.

Texture The sharp, steel-like acidity leaves the mouth feeling clean and refreshed.

The pronounced acidity – which can make the wine feel austere to the uninitiated – is a product of the relatively cool climate (since more acid remains in grapes that are grown in cooler sites or years) and the soil.

"Invigoratingly fresh Chardonnay with a steely, mineral kick."

2 SANCERRE
Loire Valley, France

Sancerre is at its best 1–2 years after the vintage

Appearance Bright, silvery white with green tints.

The pale colour hints at the wine's youth and the relatively cool climate of the Loire.

Aroma A distinctive and quite intense "green" quality: nettles, grass, gooseberries, plus elderflower and fresh citrus fruit.

These are classic Sauvignon Blanc aromas, but unlike the more pungent styles from New Zealand, Sancerre is generally more restrained, more mineral, less tropical-fruity.

Flavour Echoing the nose, with tangy gooseberry, elderflower cordial, lemon, and white grapefruit, and a touch of wet-stone minerality.

In order to preserve the grapes' pure fruit flavours, most Sancerre is made in steel tanks or old, oak barrels that have been used for several vintages and which do not impart the toasty flavours of new oak barrels.

Texture Juicy and vibrant in the mouth, with a crisp, citrusy acidity.

The best Sancerre feels vividly bright thanks to the natural acidity of Sauvignon Blanc – a quality that makes it, like lemon juice, a fine match for seafood.

"Vividly grassy, zesty, and mineral Sauvignon Blanc."

3 RIESLING
Mosel, Germany

Appearance Water-white with a touch of silver.

That very pale colour shows this is a very light and youthful wine from a cool climate – the Mosel Valley is in the more northerly reaches of European wine production.

Aroma Gently penetrating with lively floral notes, ripe orchard fruit (from apricot to apple) and lime.

The Riesling grape variety gives wines that are full of the joys of spring when young. As they age, they take on flavours akin to petrol.

Flavour Juicy peach, apricot, and ripe apple along with a squeeze of lime; a touch of slate-like wet stone.

The cool, stony flavour underlying good Mosel Riesling is credited to the slate soil of the precipitously steep vineyards, although this is far from proven scientifically.

Texture Delicate, light, and racy with a fine acidity that twangs like a steel guitar string.

Classic off-dry Mosel Riesling's distinctive texture comes from its fine balance of high acidity, light alcohol (7.5–10%), and a cushion of sweetness from stopping the fermentation before all the sugar turns to alcohol.

"Delicately fruity, gently sweet and racy."

Weingut Max Ferd. Richter
D-54486 MÜLHEIM/MOSEL

Familienbesitz seit 1680

2007

alc. 8.5% vol

Graacher Himmelreich
Riesling Kabinett

750 ml

Prädikatswein · A.P.Nr. 2 593 049 07 08

MOSEL-SAAR-RUWER

Graacher Himmelreich is a famous vineyard in the Mosel

4 ALBARIÑO
Rías Baixas, Spain

Castrocelta is a partnership of 20 grape growers and winemakers

 Appearance Bright, pale yellow-gold.

Another youthful white: the pale colour also suggests that no oak barrels have been involved in its production.

 Aroma Full of ripe peaches and apricots with very subtle notes of white flowers.

This is a high-quality example, so the aromas are like fresh fruit. In less skilled hands, they can become more like tinned peaches.

 Flavour As with the nose, there is the sense of perfectly ripe peaches and apricots with a subtle salty/mineral touch.

The classic nose of the Albariño grape. The grapes for this wine grow in a climate that benefits from the cooling breezes from the nearby Atlantic Ocean, helping to keep acidity and therefore freshness and mineral flavours in the grapes.

 Texture Cool, fresh, and round in the mouth, with the fleshiness of a ripe white peach.

The grapes were fermented in steel tanks at cold temperatures to retain freshness, but spent a little time in contact with the dead yeast cells after fermentation to give a rounded feel.

"Ripe, peachy but fresh Atlantic white."

97

Loimer is a top producer in Austria's Kamptal region

5 GRÜNER VELTLINER
Austria

Appearance Pale straw-yellow with green and silver tints in colour.

The colour suggests an unoaked and youthful wine.

Aroma Very subtle green apple aromas, with apricot, citrus, and honeyed almonds.

These are the classic aromas of the Grüner Veltliner grape variety, which is the most widely planted grape in Austria but is only just beginning to be planted elsewhere.

Flavour Zesty citrus fruit and spicy herbal, quite savoury with a touch of celery and white pepper.

Again, classic Grüner Veltliner flavours – the white pepper is a tell-tale sign of the variety.

Texture Crisp, dry, and fresh in the mouth, with a lingering white-pepper spicy and herbal finish.

Some Grüners are made in a much more ripe and powerful style. For this style, the winemaker has been careful to pick the grapes early when there is less sugar and more acidity in the grapes.

"Distinctive herbal and white-pepper flavours."

6 SOAVE
Italy

Appearance Bright, pale straw-yellow in colour.

The colour suggests this is another youthful, unoaked wine.

Aroma Very subtle green apple aromas, with apricot, citrus, and honeyed almonds.

Soave is generally a blend of the Garganega and Trebbiano grapes, occasionally with a bit of Chardonnay. Whatever the components, the best Soave always has that distinctive almond note.

Flavour Vibrant, rich lemon and apple with soft apricot and that slightly honeyed almond flavour.

A lot of Soave is rather bland, almost neutral. The better examples, however, come from older vines (30 years old or more) in the higher-quality vineyards of the Soave Classico zone, which gives them much more flavour.

Texture Gently rounded but with a feeling of freshness and lightness.

Soave is never powerful or rich in texture, but the best versions do not feel dilute, again thanks to careful work in the vineyards, where the producer has avoided growing too many grape bunches per vine, meaning the grapes have a greater concentration of sugar, minerals, and acidity.

The Inama family has helped raised the quality image of the Soave region

"Graceful, soft, lemon-fresh white with a touch of almond."

Choosing Your Wine

You have now taken the first few steps in your vinous journey through the classic white wines of Europe. You should now be able to see how different countries and different regions take varying approaches to winemaking, producing a wide range of flavours and styles.

1 CHABLIS
Burgundy, France

This cool-climate northern French region produces bone-dry Chardonnays that are marked by a distinctive steely acidity and flinty mineral character with little or no oaky flavour.

Buying advice The best examples come from top vineyard sites labelled Premier Cru or Grand Cru – these can age beautifully for up to 20 years.
Food pairing Chablis is a classic match with oysters and other shellfish.
Also try Unoaked Chardonnays from Australia or New Zealand. Or compare and contrast with a richer, oak-aged Chardonnay from further south in Burgundy such as Mersault.

2 SANCERRE
Loire Valley, France

The spiritual home of the Sauvignon Blanc grape variety makes vividly pure and refreshing wines that combine restrained "green" grassy and gooseberry flavours with citrus acidity and mineral flavours.

Buying advice Most Sancerre is best consumed young, within 1 to 3 years of the vintage. The villages of Bue or Chavignol are often good quality.
Food pairing Seafood and fish works well, but it's also a fine match for young goat's cheese.

Also try Sauvignons from other Loire Valley regions such as Pouilly-Fumé, Menetou-Salon, Quincy, Reuilly, and Touraine.

3 RIESLING
Mosel, Germany

Delicate and elegant without being wimpy or weak, these light alcohol off-dry wines have a racy quality that comes from their fine, steel-wire-like acidity, and graceful floral and orchard fruit aromas.

Buying advice Look for wines marked as *Kabinett* on the label for the delicate off-dry style. Labels featuring the word *trocken* indicate a dry style, which can be equally as good as the off-dry.
Food pairing Sushi or grilled fresh river fish such as trout. Light garden salads.
Also try Delicate Rieslings from other parts of Germany, such as the Nahe, Rheingau, and Rheinhessen.

4 ALBARIÑO
Rías Baixas, Spain

From vineyards in the heart of Galicia in España Verde (or Green Spain) in the country's northern coastal region, Albariño makes for gorgeously peachy and floral aromatic whites with a rounded, fleshy but fresh texture.

Sauvignon Blanc grapes *growing in a vineyard in the Sancerre appellation, France.*

Buying advice Although some examples do age, most Albariño is best consumed young, within two to three years of the vintage.

Food pairing Serving Albariño with seafood is the traditional Spanish combination, but this wine also complements simple white meat such as grilled chicken.

Also try Other Galician whites such as those made from the Godello variety in Valdeorras. Or head across the border to northern Portugal, where the grape variety is known as Alvarinho.

5 GRÜNER VELTLINER
Austria

These sophisticated, complex, but utterly drinkable whites with characteristic flavours of wild herbs, orchard fruit, and white pepper are made from Austria's most widely planted grape variety.

Buying advice Look for the three great eastern Austrian regions of Kamptal, Wachau, and Kremstal.

Food pairing White meat dishes, such as chicken in tarragon sauce. The herbal flavours can also work well with mildly spicy Vietnamese salads with mint and coriander.

Also try Grüner Veltliner is rarely found outside Austria. For similar flavours and styles, look to dry Rieslings from Austria, Alsace (France), Australia, and the Pfalz (Germany).

6 SOAVE
Italy

This is a light, dry, softly fruity white from the Soave zone in the northeastern Italian region of Veneto. Generally a blend of the local Garganega grape with Trebbiano and sometimes Chardonnay, the wines have a gentle almond flavour.

Buying advice Look for wines from vineyards in the best sites at the heart of the Soave by looking at the labels – the wines you want will be called Soave Classico.

Food pairing Seafood risotto and pasta dishes. Salads and vegetable dishes.

Also try Pinot Grigio from northeastern Italian region Friuli, Verdicchio from Italy's Adriatic coast, or a lighter white Burgundy such as Mâcon.

Explore

Classic European Reds

As with the continent's white wine styles, European reds
are the originals, the styles against which winemakers
around the world measure their work. In this tasting we'll
be looking at six of the most celebrated regions.

Blends of strength

In our tour of the classic European whites
(see pp.90–101) we saw that European
wines are frequently labelled by region
rather than grape variety. This is just as
much the case with reds as whites, and
part of the reason is that many classic
European wines use multiple grape
varieties in their wines. That's certainly the
case in the region that is arguably Europe's,
and indeed the world's, most famous red-
wine region – Bordeaux. Here winemakers
will use a combination of Cabernet
Sauvignon and Merlot grapes in varying
proportions, along with greater or lesser
proportions of Cabernet Franc and Petit
Verdot. These different grapes provide
different flavours and textural elements to
the finished wine, and even the precise
blend will vary from producer to producer.

Much the same happens in France's
southern Rhône Valley, where the famous
Châteauneuf-du-Pape appellation, located
near Avignon, permits some 18 different
grape varieties. Similarly, the fine reds of
Portugal's Douro Valley are allowed more
than 100 different varieties.

Dominant singles

Elsewhere in Europe, some regions are
strongly associated with a single grape
variety. Tuscany, Italy – in the Chianti,
Brunello di Montalcino, and Vino Nobile di
Montepulciano zones – is the land of
Sangiovese, although it is usually blended
with a small proportion of other varieties.
Tempranillo, again generally blended with
one or more other varieties, is the king
of Spanish regions Rioja and Ribera de
Duero.Likewise, Burgundy in France is
synonymous with pure Pinot Noir, and the
Barolo and Barberesco zones in Piedmont,
northern Italy, are all about Nebbiolo.

At their best, Europe's classic red wines
all have a distinct sense of place, expressing
the combination of land, local culture,
climate, and grape variety (or varieties)
that is unique to its geographical area.

In Tuscany *Sangiovese is the dominant grape*
variety and is grown throughout the region.

Tasting Session

1 BURGUNDY
France

Made from the fickle, thin-skinned Pinot Noir grape variety, Burgundy's red wines are all about subtle, perfumed, silky elegance.

Look for Joseph Drouhin Laforêt Bourgogne Rouge; Domaine Faiveley Bourgogne Hautes-Côtes de Nuits Dames Hugettes

Serve at
13–16°C
(55–61°F)

Grape Variety
Pinot Noir

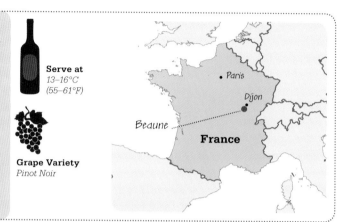

2 BORDEAUX
France

Made from a blend of grapes usually dominated by either Cabernet Sauvignon or Merlot, Bordeaux's famously long-lived reds marry firm structure with elegance.

Look for Château Ormes de Pez or L'Ermitage de Chasse-Spleen, two well-priced, quality estates

Serve at
16–18°C
(61–64°F)

Grape Varieties
Merlot, Cabernet Sauvignon, Cabernet Franc, Petit Verdot

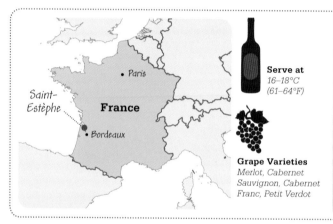

3 RHÔNE VALLEY
France

France's Rhône Valley makes rich, spicy, and warming reds with a supple texture and savoury and peppery character.

Look for Domaine de la Janasse Côtes du Rhône; Château Sainte-Cosme Gigondas; Château La Nerthe Châteauneuf-du-Pape

Serve at
16–18°C
(61–64°F)

Grape Varieties
Syrah, Grenache, Mourvèdre, Carignan, Cinsault

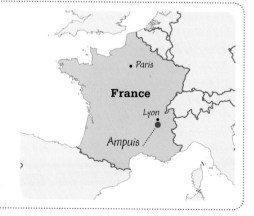

4 CHIANTI
Italy

The Tuscan grape Sangiovese dominates the blend of wines made in Chianti, making lively, medium-bodied reds with flavours of red cherries, plums, and herbs.

Look for Castello di Volpaia Chianti Classico; Fontodi Chianti Classico

Serve at
16–18°C
(61–64°F)

Grape Varieties
Sangiovese, Caniolo, Colorino, Cabernet Sauvignon, Merlot

Florence
Radda in Chianti
Rome
Italy

5 BAROLO
Italy

Tough and tannic in their youth, Barolo's powerful reds made from the Nebbiolo grape increase in elegance as they age, with notes of plum, roses, tar, and liquorice.

Look for wines by GD Vajra, Giacomo Conterno, and Bruno Giacosa

Turin
Barolo
Rome
Italy

Serve at
16–18°C
(61–64°F)

Grape Variety
Nebbiolo

6 RIOJA
Spain

Soft, smooth, and warming reds, Riojas have a distinctive coconut and vanilla character derived from long periods spent ageing in American oak barrels.

Look for CVNE Rioja Reserva or Muga Rioja Reserva – wines from two traditional bodegas (wineries)

Serve at
16–18°C
(61–64°F)

Grape Varieties
Tempranillo, Garnacha, Graciano, Mazuelo

Haro
Vitoria
Madrid
Spain

1 BURGUNDY
France

Appearance Pale but bright ruby-red with purple tinges.

The thin-skinned Pinot Noir grape variety, particularly when grown in a cool climate such as Burgundy in northern France, makes wines with a paler colour than those made with thicker-skinned varieties.

Aroma Delicate, ethereal. Notes of red fruit – cherry, raspberry, a touch floral.

Pinot Noir is sensitive to where it is grown, and nowhere is that more apparent than in Burgundy, where even adjacent vines will produce grapes with very different aromas and flavours.

Flavour More of those subtle, succulent red fruits, occasionally almost tomato-like in some, a little more dark-berried in others. Forest floor, wild mushroom.

The intensity and character of the flavour varies greatly among Burgundy's many villages and appellations. The best are labelled Grand Cru or Premier Cru.

Texture Light-to-medium-bodied, with a silky, supple texture. It has an abiding feeling of freshness.

The silky mouthfeel and freshness comes from a balance of light but ripe tannins and good acidity. Burgundy is very vintage-dependent, and in bad (cool, wet) years, the wines can cross over into the sour and tart.

The producer's name is the best guide to quality in Burgundy

Joseph Drouhin

LAFORET

BOURGOGNE
Appellation Bourgogne Contrôlée

PINOT NOIR

Mis en bouteille par France, aux Celliers des Rois de

Joseph Drouhin à Beaune, France et des Ducs de Bourgogne

12,5% vol.   PRODUIT DE FRANCE   750 ml

"Ethereal, elegantly silky reds from the Pinot Noir grape variety."

This wine, labelled Bourgogne, uses grapes from vineyards across the region

2 BORDEAUX
France

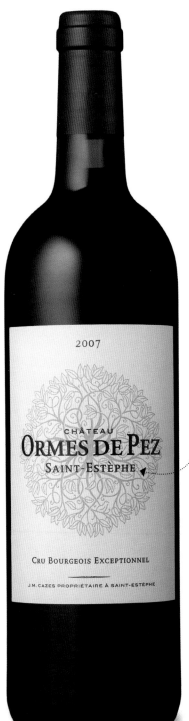

2007

CHÂTEAU
ORMES DE PEZ
SAINT-ESTÈPHE

Bordeaux has many sub-regions, such as St-Estèphe

CRU BOURGEOIS EXCEPTIONNEL

J.M. CAZES PROPRIÉTAIRE À SAINT-ESTÈPHE

Appearance Deep purple in youth fading to ruby and garnet as it ages.

The word claret is often used as a synonym for Bordeaux red wines. It comes from the French word clairet, *which historically described the wines' raspberry-red colour.*

Aroma Cassis, cedar wood, and pencil lead; tobacco and leather with age.

The aromas and flavours vary greatly depending on the balance of grape varieties used in the blend. More Cabernet Sauvignon brings more cassis, Merlot fleshy plums.

Flavour A core of fresh red and black fruits leading to complex flavours of tobacco, cedar wood, chocolate, and leather, particularly in older wines.

The best red Bordeaux develop really well with age, when "secondary" characters (the more savoury flavours described above) take over from the bright "primary" black fruit.

Texture In youth, they can feel tough and astringent. Older wines feel soft and harmonious; middleweight, with a long, haunting finish.

The best Bordeaux need time to soften and harmonize, and may improve for decades.

"Harmonious reds that mellow gracefully with age."

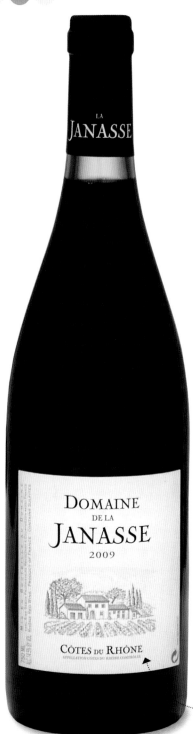

3 RHÔNE VALLEY
France

Appearance Varies, from bright deep ruby-red to dark black cherry.

The colour is influenced by the blend: Grenache is quite thin-skinned, giving lighter-coloured wines; Syrah and Mourvèdre are thick-skinned, giving much darker colours.

Aroma Quite intense, soft, ripe red and black fruit, black pepper, wild herbs such as rosemary and thyme.

The black pepper notes and black fruit are typical of Syrah; the ripe red fruit is common to Grenache. The herbal notes are distinctive of the region.

Flavour Following the nose, maybe with some savoury flavours: meat and leather.

The Rhône has two distinct regions. In the south, reds are usually blends of varieties and have soft red fruit. In the north, the wines are made from Syrah, and have distinctive flavours of blackberries, black pepper, and tar.

Texture Medium to full-bodied and generous. Soft, mellow, and warming in the mouth, with a slight gripping sensation.

The texture of a Rhône red depends on the varieties used. Southern blends are usually higher in alcohol than northern Syrahs.

Wines labelled Côtes du Rhône can use grapes grown throughout the Rhône region

4 CHIANTI
Italy

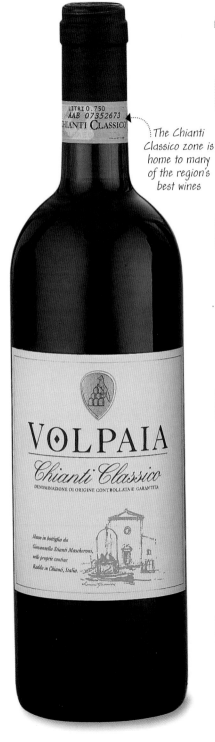

The Chianti Classico zone is home to many of the region's best wines

Appearance Ruby-red with a touch of garnet as it ages.

Wines made from the Sangiovese grape were traditionally much lighter than today – producers used to blend it with white grapes, a practice far less common now.

Aroma Gently insinuating rather than loudly insistent. Notes of red cherries – fresh and dried – oregano, cloves, and leather.

These are the classic aromas of Sangiovese. Some modern Chianti will also have notes of darker fruit such as cassis, the result of including a little of the strongly flavoured Cabernet Sauvignon in the blend.

Flavour Following the nose in terms of character. The wine feels brisk, tangy – with a little hint of bitter blood orange – yet savoury.

The best Chianti tends to come from vineyards between Siena and Florence, an area officially demarcated as Chianti Classico, and in the Chianti Rufina zone to the east of Florence, where those tangy flavours are beautifully balanced and concentrated.

Texture Very dry and gently astringent. Medium-bodied.

Sangiovese grapes have naturally high levels of tannin and acidity, which is reflected in the wine's gentle astringency.

5 BAROLO
Italy

The seal for the Barolo zone which, along with neighbouring Barbaresco, produces the world's best Nebbiolo......

Appearance Pale ruby with a brick-like tinge.

The Nebbiolo grape variety is not high in pigment. The wines also spend quite a long time in barrel and bottle before release – at least three years, with two of those in barrel – which brings more brick-like colours.

Aroma Mute at first, over time Barolo develops distinctive notes of roses, tar, liquorice, and truffles, as well as raspberry, plum, and cherry.

The Nebbiolo grape is thought to have taken its name from the Italian word for fog – nebbia – which shrouds the Piedmontese hills in autumn when the late-ripening Nebbiolo approaches harvest.

Flavour Mature Barolo is ethereal – the taste of roses and truffles is gentle, delicate, elusive.

Nebbiolo grown in Barolo is powerful (high alcohol, tannin, and acidity) yet delicate (subtle floral and savoury flavours).

Texture Astringent – very high acidity and tannin.

The distinctive Nebbiolo character comes from tough skins high in tannin and polyphenols. Some modern producers have begun to use smaller, new oak barrels and shorter fermentations to make the tannins feel softer, but Barolo will always be marked by the high tannin and acidity of the Nebbiolo grape.

6 RIOJA
Spain

Appearance Intense garnet fading to ruby and terracotta in older wines.

Rioja wines spend a long time ageing in oak barrels and bottles before release – the longer the time in barrel, the more the colour moves towards terracotta or brick.

Aroma Strawberries, coconut, vanilla, plum, tobacco, and leather.

Many of these aromas are the product of Rioja's long ageing period, which traditionally uses American white oak barrels, which impart sweeter flavours such as coconut and vanilla.

By law a Rioja Reserva must spend at least three years ageing in barrel and bottle before being released ...

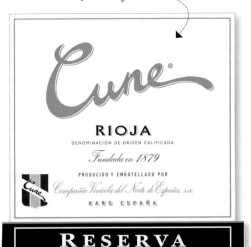

Flavour Following the nose with more complex, savoury flavours such as leather, tobacco, and dried fruit such as figs, particularly in older wines.

You can get a good indication about the style of Rioja from the label. A wine marked Jovén (or "young") will be full of youthful black fruit, having spent little or no time in oak barrels. As bottles move through the officially defined Crianza, Reserva, and Gran Reserva categories, they will have spent progressively more time in barrel and bottle, and the flavours will move from the more obviously fresh and fruity to the more savoury.

Texture Soft, mellow, smooth, long.

Tannins and acidity always soften after time, as the wine interacts with oxygen. Because Rioja Crianza, Reserva, and Gran Reserva wines are generally released much later than most red wines, they have a much softer, more mellow feel.

"Smooth, mellow, oak-influenced reds from northwest Spain"

Choosing Your Wine

Classic European red wines have evolved over centuries, often hand-in-hand with the local cuisine. In recent years the influence of ideas from the New World has brought some changes to classic winemaking approaches, but the techniques and grape varieties used are strictly controlled by local wine laws designed to protect tradition.

A good, classic European red *is the product of centuries of winemaking tradition.*

1 BURGUNDY
France

These elegant, silky, complex reds are made from the Pinot Noir grape in the many different appellations of the Burgundy region.

Buying advice With so many different village and vineyard names featuring on bottles, buying Burgundy can be hit-and-miss, and expensive. Find a wine merchant you trust to help and for cheaper styles try regional appellations such as Bourgogne Rouge, Hauts-Côtes de Nuit, or Côtes de Beaune.
Food pairing Richer styles work beautifully with duck and game meat. Lighter styles are perfect with salmon and other meaty fish.
Also try Pinot Noir from Sancerre in the Loire Valley, Germany (where it is known as Spätburgunder), or Oregon in the Pacific Northwest of the USA.

2 BORDEAUX
France

Made from blends of grape varieties dominated by either Cabernet Sauvignon or Merlot, Bordeaux's middleweight reds combine cassis and pencil-lead flavours with noticeable tannin and acidity that softens remarkably over time. Outside France, these Bordeaux reds (and occasionally some Bordeaux-style reds) are also widely known as "clarets".

Buying advice The top wines, known as the first growths, are expensive. For more accessible prices look for lower-ranking classifications, such as Cru Bourgeois, or less famous appellations such as Côtes de Castillon or Côtes de Bourg, on the label.

Food pairing Most claret works beautifully with roasts of red meat such as lamb or beef.

Also try Compare and contrast with wines made from the same grape varieties in California, Australia, Chile, or neighbouring Bergerac.

3 RHÔNE VALLEY
France

The Rhône Valley in southeastern France produces two distinct styles of wine: warming, generous blends lead by Syrah and Grenache in the south; spicy, sinewy 100% Syrahs in the north.

Buying advice Great value can be found in the Côtes du Rhône appellation; for more complex examples look to Châteauneuf-du-Pape, Gigondas, Cairanne or Rasteau in the south or Côte-Rôtie, Crozes-Hermitage, or Cornas in the north.

Food pairing Try these wines with intensely flavoured casseroles, or herb-roasted red meat.

Also try Look for Shiraz and/or Grenache-based wines in Spain's Priorat, France's Languedoc, Australia's Barossa Valley, and California.

4 CHIANTI
Italy

These are medium-bodied, food-friendly reds from the heart of Tuscany with flavours of cherries and herbs, some savoury notes, and refreshing astringency.

Buying advice For the best quality look for wines produced in the zones of Chianti Classico and Chianti Rufina.

Food pairing Pasta with meat or tomato ragu. Tuscan T-bone steak.

Also try Other Tuscan wines made from Sangiovese such as Vino Nobile di Montepulciano or powerful Brunello di Montalcino.

5 BAROLO
Italy

Made from the Nebbiolo grape variety in the hills of Piedmont, Barolo is tough and astringent in its youth, but ages beautifully, taking on complex flavours of tar, plum, cherry, roses, and truffles.

Buying advice Many Barolos have a short window of drinking opportunity: the old adage says you should wait for ten years after the vintage, and then drink within 15 years.

Food pairing Local cuisine such as wild mushroom risotto or pasta.

Also try Nebbiolo from neighbouring Barbaresco; or Aglianico from Basilicata and Campania in southern Italy.

6 RIOJA
Spain

Soft, mellow and made from the Tempranillo grape in the northern Spanish region of the same name, traditional Rioja is characterized by its gentle coconut and vanilla flavours. Some modern Riojas are much richer with darker fruit.

Buying advice Look for Gran Reserva for the traditional style; newer styles are often simply labelled Rioja.

Food pairing Roast pork or lamb; hard cheeses.

Also try Look to neighbouring Ribera del Duero and Toro for powerful examples of Tempranillo.

Explore

Classic New World Whites

Europe may have tradition on its side, but wine producers
in the so-called New World countries of Australasia, the
Americas, and South Africa have caught up fast,
developing modern-day classics of their own.

New World winemakers burst on the global scene in the late 20th century. They developed a reputation for experimentation, in grape varieties (planting whatever they liked, wherever they liked) and in winemaking techniques that tended to be more technical, scientific, and hygienic. A "New World style" evolved: wines made from one grape variety, grown in warm climates, with bold, rich, ripe, and obviously fruity flavours. Many European winemakers now use New World techniques, and many in the New World look to Europe in seeking to add more subtlety, finesse, and regional character. Even so, the best of the New World wines are still marked by the generosity of fruit flavour that has won over so many drinkers all over the world.

Vineyards *in the Marlborough region, New Zealand.*

Windsor

San Francisco

California, U.S.

Los Angeles

Serve at
*10–12°C
(50–54°F)*

Grape Variety
Chardonnay

1 CHARDONNAY
California, USA
North America's largest wine-producing state makes full-flavoured styles known for their ripe, sunny fruit and rich texture.

Look for Sonoma Cutrer, Sonoma Coast Chardonnay; Bonterra Vineyards Chardonnay, Mendocino County

Tasting Session

2 SAUVIGNON BLANC
New Zealand

Though Sauvignon Blanc vines were only planted in New Zealand in the 1970s, the country is now synonymous with pungent, vibrantly fruity examples of this variety.

Look for Blind River Sauvignon Blanc; Villa Maria Private Bin Sauvignon Blanc

Serve at
10–12°C
(50–54°F)

Grape Variety
Sauvignon Blanc

South Island, New Zealand

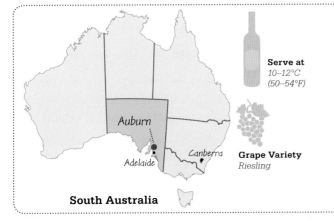

South Australia

Serve at
10–12°C
(50–54°F)

Grape Variety
Riesling

3 RIESLING
South Australia

Australia is perhaps best known for Chardonnay, but in the Clare and Eden Valleys of South Australia it has developed a uniquely crisp, dry, and limey style of Riesling.

Look for Grosset Springvale Riesling; Tim Adams, Clare Valley Riesling

---

4 CHENIN BLANC
South Africa

Frequently known here by the local name Steen, this is the most widely planted variety in South Africa, and is made in a variety of styles, from crisp and dry to rich and full.

Look for Cederberg Chenin Blanc; Bellingham Old Vine Series Chenin Blanc

Serve at
10–12°C
(50–54°F)

Grape Variety
Chenin Blanc

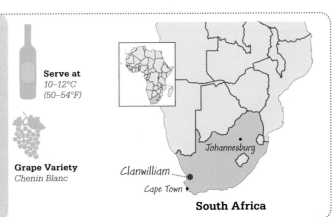

South Africa

1 CHARDONNAY
California, USA

Appearance Bright yellow-gold.

Californians tend to make Chardonnay in a rich style, using fully ripe grapes and ageing the wine in new oak barrels, which both contribute to its golden colour.

Aroma Intense, ripe tropical fruit: pineapple, melon, banana.

California has many different growing regions, with subtle variations in climate and soil. As a rule of thumb, the closer to the coast, where the morning fog rolls off the Pacific Ocean, the cooler the site and the fresher the wines.

Flavour Lots of intense ripe tropical fruit with a touch of butter, toast, and vanilla.

Californian Chardonnay is usually fermented in barrels, with bâtonnage (stirring barrels of wine to keep the wine in contact with dead yeast cells). This style of winemaking creates buttery and toasty flavours.

Texture Full-bodied, almost viscous.

California Chardonnays are always ripe and full in texture, but in recent years the best have become much more restrained, the result of both seeking out cooler climates and using a lighter touch in the winery.

Many of California's best Chardonnays are produced in the Sonoma region

"Rich and hedonistic, like the golden Californian sun."

The Blind River winery uses a Maori-style motif of an eel on its bottles

2 SAUVIGNON BLANC
New Zealand

Appearance Bright pale-straw with a hint of green.

This is the typical colour of Sauvignon Blanc that has been made in stainless steel tanks rather than oak barrels.

Aroma A vivid, pungent mix of elderflower, gooseberry, passionfruit, and mango, with a touch of grassiness.

Most of New Zealand's Sauvignon Blanc comes from the Marlborough region in the South Island. A slightly warmer climate and more dazzling sunshine than Sancerre in France (see p.95) produces wines with a slightly more tropical profile.

Flavour More of those pungent tropical and green flavours, with an underlying lemon-and-lime freshness. Dry.

Winemakers in New Zealand often like to blend grapes of different ripeness levels. Some are picked earlier when they have more citrus and green flavours and higher acidity; others are picked later, when they have more sugar and tropical fruit flavours.

Texture Zippy and fresh; medium-bodied.

Marlborough has a long growing season, but the climate is moderated by cooling onshore breezes that help preserve acidity in the grapes and therefore freshness in the wines.

BLIND RIVER
MARLBOROUGH
2010
SAUVIGNON BLANC

3 RIESLING
Australia

Appearance Pale yellow with a tint of silver and green.

The Riesling grape takes on a richer, more golden hue as it ages.

Aroma Intense lime with touches of peach and pineapple.

Australia's finest Riesling is made in the Clare Valley, north of Adelaide in South Australia, where a continental climate (warm days but very cool nights) gives a more intense character than the cooler sites of Riesling's homeland in Germany.

Jeffrey Grosset is a specialist in Riesling in the Clare Valley region

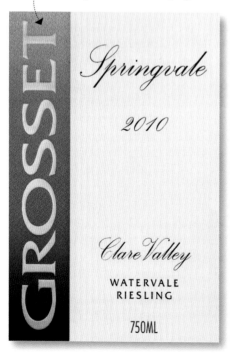

Grosset
Springvale
2010
Clare Valley
WATERVALE
RIESLING
750ML

Flavour More of that lime, plus a toasty character as it ages.

Clare Valley Rieslings are always without oak influence, with cool fermentations in stainless steel to preserve the crisp, precise flavours. The winemakers here were among the first to pioneer screwcaps rather than corks, believing that the screwcap did a better job of preserving freshness.

Texture Very racy and elegant – extremely tangy acidity makes them mouthwatering.

Riesling is a grape that is naturally high in acidity, but the texture of these wines varies depending on where the grapes are grown within the valley. The limestone soils of the area around Watervale in the south make wines that are more abundantly lime-juicy. The slate soils of Polish Hill are leaner, with more mineral (wet stone) flavours. The high acidity, which acts as a preservative, makes these wines very long-lived (two decades and more), taking on toast, caraway seed, and petrol-like aromas as they mature.

"Zingy, precise, limey, dry Rieslings."

4 CHENIN BLANC
South Africa

Appearance Pale straw to gold.

South African Chenin Blanc is made in a number of styles: the lighter colour indicates a crisp, light style that has seen no oak; the more golden coloured are likely to have been aged in small French oak barrels.

Aroma Quince, hay, baked apples or apple pie, honey.

These are the classic aromas of the Chenin Blanc grape variety which performs well in South African regions such as Stellenbosch, Swartland, and Paarl.

Flavour Rich, slightly honeyed – baked hay and apples.

The best South African Chenin Blanc is made from very old vines (50 years or more), which produce fewer bunches per vine, yielding more concentrated, layered fruit flavours.

Texture Full-bodied and dry, almost waxy.

Like Chardonnay, Chenin Blanc responds well to careful oak ageing and lees stirring (see p.116). Many of the most intense South African Chenin Blancs are also made with more contact with the skins after pressing the grapes, giving a richer feel.

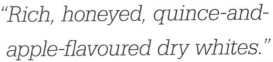

"Rich, honeyed, quince-and-apple-flavoured dry whites."

Choosing Your Wine

Classic New World whites may have started out as imitations of European originals but over the years they have developed into distinctive styles in their own right, with their own signature. They are evolving all the time as winemakers discover the locations that are best suited to different grape varieties.

A glass or two of chilled white wine *can rarely be surpassed on a hot summer's day.*

1 CHARDONNAY
California, USA
Rich and full of tropical fruit and with a round, rich almost viscous texture, these are Chardonnays with the flavour dialled up high and with an inviting sun-filled generosity of texture.

Buying advice Avoid the cheaper end: many of Calfornia's high-volume brands can be overly sweet and clumsy, lacking in freshness.
Food pairing The richness works well with pork or buttery roast chicken.
Also try Rich, dry Chardonnays from Australia, Chile and Washington State in the USA; Californian Viognier.

2 SAUVIGNON BLANC
New Zealand
Vibrantly aromatic, verdant, and full of passion fruit, gooseberry, and tropical fruit, New Zealand's Sauvignon Blanc is also crisp and clean with citrus acidity.

Buying advice It is best drunk young when it still has all its vibrant youthful aromas; drink within a year or two of the vintage.
Food pairing Works very well with seafood and fish, and the extra fruit flavours also match well with mildly spicy Asian flavours.
Also try Compare and contrast with a Sauvignon Blanc from France's Loire Valley or South Africa.

3 RIESLING
South Australia

Zesty and full of freshly squeezed lime notes, Australian Riesling is unoaked, dry, pure, and very fresh: stimulating your tongue with its nervy acidity, it takes on toasty aromas as it ages.

Buying advice Look for wines from the Clare Valley or the nearby Eden Valley in South Australia.
Food pairing Try it with shellfish or a summer garden salad.
Also try Compare and contrast with Riesling from Alsace or Germany's Pfalz region; Hunter Valley Sémillon from New South Wales, another unique Australian that ages well.

4 CHENIN BLANC
South Africa

Made in a variety of styles from the crisp and dry to the honeyed and rich, Chenin Blanc is South Africa's most important grape, with a long pedigree in that country.

Buying advice Chenin Blanc from South Africa is often good value. Look to the back label for an indication of style: the richer examples are usually barrel-aged or fermented.
Food pairing Richer styles work well with buttery roast chicken and pork; lighter, crisper styles are better with fish.
Also try It's fun to compare a Cape Chenin Blanc with an example from California or France; also try Marsanne and Roussanne wines from Australia and California.

Wine growers *have to know just when to harvest the grapes in order to produce the best wines.*

Explore

Classic New World Reds

Just as they have done with white wines, producers in the
New World have taken classic European grape varieties
and moulded them into new, bolder shapes – as you taste
the wines, look out for their stronger fruit flavours.

South Africa's *Stellenbosch wine-growing region.*

Wine has been made in the so-called New World for centuries, but the first country to emerge on the global stage was the USA, in the 1970s, in particular California's Napa Valley with its intensely flavoured Cabernet Sauvignons, now widely regarded as some of the world's finest red wines. Australia took off in the 1980s with even richer, denser red wines made from Syrah, known in Australia as Shiraz. New Zealand did the same with its Sauvignon Blanc whites and, in the 1990s, its fruity Pinot Noir. Argentina, had a quality revolution in the 1990s, and became synonymous with Malbec. These countries make other styles, as do Chile and South Africa, but the wines chosen for this tasting all exemplify how the New World has adapted European ingredients.

Oakville

San Francisco

California, U.S.

Los Angeles

Serve at
16–18°C
(61–64°F)

Grape Variety
Cabernet Sauvignon

1 CABERNET SAUVIGNON
California, USA
This grape variety from Bordeaux is grown across California, but hits its zenith in the Napa Valley north of San Francisco, where it makes powerful, richly textured reds.

Look for Robert Mondavi Cabernet Sauvignon Reserve; First Press Napa Valley Cabernet Sauvignon

Tasting Session

2 SHIRAZ
South Australia

Grown across Australia, in the very warm Barossa Valley and McLaren Vale in South Australia, this grape makes powerful wines dense with flavours of sweet black fruit.

Look for Two Hands Gnarly Dudes Shiraz, Barossa Valley; Château Reynella Basket Pressed Shiraz

Serve at
16–18°C
(61–64°F)

Grape Variety
Shiraz

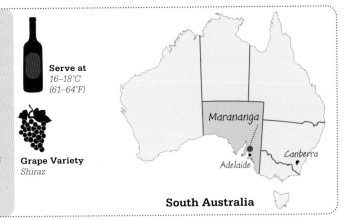

South Australia

3 PINOT NOIR
New Zealand

New Zealand is one of the few regions outside Burgundy to have some success with the Pinot Noir variety, making succulently smooth, fruity examples.

Look for Mt Difficulty Roaring Meg Pinot Noir; Churton Pinot Noir, Marlborough

Serve at
14–16°C
(57–61°F)

Grape Variety
Pinot Noir

South Island, New Zealand

4 MALBEC
Argentina

The foothills of the Andes in Mendoza province are an ideal place for the Malbec grape from Bordeaux, making fleshy, perfumed wines with lots of backbone.

Look for Altos Las Hormigas Malbec; Achaval Ferrer Malbec; Catena Zapata Malbec

Serve at
16–18°C
(61–64°F)

Grape Variety
Malbec

Argentina

1 CABERNET SAUVIGNON
California, USA

Appearance Deep dark purple-red in colour.

The sign of fully ripe grapes from the thick-skinned Cabernet Sauvignon variety grown in the warm California climate.

Aroma Intense aromas of black fruit (blackcurrant and blackberry), coffee, vanilla.

The long, warm, dry summers and luminous sunshine of California are perfectly suited to the late-ripening Cabernet, helping it to develop intense fruit aromas.

Flavour More of that concentrated black fruit with complex savoury notes of black olive. Vanilla, coffee, and toast in young wines; more leather and cigar-box as they age.

The vanilla and coffee notes are a sign of new French oak barrels used in the winemaking. In the past, many Californian wines were dominated by these flavours, but winemakers have learnt to use them with a much more sensitive touch so that they feel integrated rather than jarring.

Texture Rich, full-bodied, but sumptuously soft.

Cabernet grapes are naturally high in tannins, but California's growing conditions mean those tannins are able to get perfectly ripe and feel wonderfully smooth.

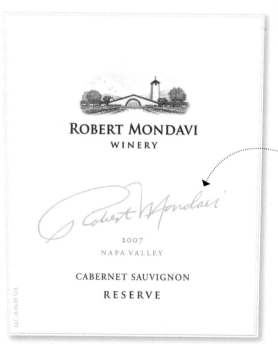

...The late Robert Mondavi, who founded this producer, was a pioneer of quality California wine

"Supercharged Cabernet Sauvignon with a voluptuous texture."

2 SHIRAZ
Australia

Appearance Dark black-purple. Almost inky.

Shiraz is a black, thick-skinned grape with lots of pigmentation. Many of the best Australian examples come from low-yielding (very few bunches per vine) old vines with smaller berries, leading to a higher skin-to-juice ratio and even darker colours.

Aroma Dark fruits, blueberries, shading to dried fruit such as prunes. Mint, eucalyptus.

The classic Australian regions of Barossa Valley and McLaren Vale are among the warmest in the world. Producers have to harvest before the aromas develop a "baked" character, where dried fruit takes over from fresher fruit.

Flavour Very intense fruit, almost like concentrated fruit juice or jam. Chocolate, a touch of smoke.

Classic Australian Shiraz divides opinion. Some find it almost too intense and jammy, and lacking finesse. Others marvel at its remarkable concentration of flavour. As with all wine, the final arbiter is personal taste.

Texture Viscous, dense, very full-bodied; soft tannins.

Accumulating lots of sugar on their way to flavour ripeness, Australian Shiraz can be very high in alcohol – often more than 15%, sometimes as high as 17.5%. This too divides opinion; how you react depends on personal taste and mood.

Australia has some of the oldest Shiraz vines in the world

T W O   H A N D S

GNARLY DUDES

"Massively concentrated and dense with fruit."

125

① ② ③

3 PINOT NOIR
New Zealand

 Appearance Bright pale ruby-cherry red.

As we saw on p.85 and p.106, thin-skinned Pinot Noir is naturally lighter in colour than other varieties and requires a gentle touch when extracting the delicate flavour and colour in the winery.

 Aroma Bright red cherry, raspberry, bergamot, and strawberry.

The classic aromas of Pinot Noir often have an extra level of fruitiness in New Zealand, which is cool in climate, but with lots of very bright sunshine – the ozone layer is very thin in this part of the southern hemisphere.

The Central Otago region has established a fine reputation for Pinot Noir

 Flavour Pure and fruity, seductive, bright and fresh.

Again, the climate is important here, with enough sunshine for the grapes to ripen flavours, and cooling onshore breezes to maintain acidity and freshness. Compared to the Pinot Noirs of Burgundy, New Zealand's are much less earthy and mineral, which is thought to be because the Pinot vines in most parts of New Zealand are very young and lack the complexity of flavour that comes from older vines.

 Texture Very silky, light and juicy. Clean texture.

A well-made Pinot Noir has a distinctive textural quality. New Zealand manages to achieve this quality much more consistently than Burgundy since it has a much more reliable climate.

"The silky luxuriance of Pinot Noir with an extra dimension of bright fruit."

4 MALBEC
Argentina

Appearance Dark purple with violet and red tints.

The Malbec grape is naturally high in pigment. Wine made from this variety in Cahors in France (where the grape is known as Côt) was known as "the black wine".

Aroma Plum, black cherry, and chocolate, sometimes with a violet-floral lift.

Most Argentinian Malbec comes from Mendoza, in the foothills of the Andes, which has vineyards at an unusually high altitude of

900m (2,950ft), often considerably higher. As a rule, the higher the vineyard, the more aromatic and well-defined the fruit flavour.

Flavour Beguilingly rich with plum and cherry leading to chocolate and vanilla.

Malbec responds well to careful oak-ageing. Some winemakers have a tendency to "over-oak" their wines, however, using new, toasted oak barrels that overwhelm the fruit characters with toasty and vanilla flavours (see p.140).

Texture Rich, warming and fleshy – structured and firm but with great freshness and length.

There is a big difference between Mendoza's day-time and night-time temperatures. The heat of the day allows Malbec grapes to ripen sugar and flavours; the drastically cooler nights helps them preserve acidity. The wines therefore balance ripe fruit flavours, ripe tannins, and freshness.

......The name of this brand – Altos las Hormigas – translates as "Ants' Heights"

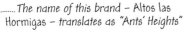

"Rich, vivacious reds from the foothills of the Andes."

Choosing Your Wine

Classic New World reds have historically tended to have a more fruit-driven, richer character than their European equivalents. However, as with all things in wine but particularly in the fast-changing New World, this is a useful generalization rather than a hard-and-fast rule and new styles are emerging all the time.

Many of the New World reds *are designed to complement rich, local meat dishes.*

1 CABERNET SAUVIGNON
California

Lush and seductively textured, made from the Cabernet Sauvignon grape variety, these wines are big-boned but beautifully balanced with smooth ripe tannins.

Buying advice The best wines from the Napa Valley can be quite expensive but, just like the best of the Bordeaux from France, they do age remarkably well.

Food pairing Beef, steak, barbecues.

Also try Cabernets from Washington State, Chile, Argentina, and Australia's Coonawarra.

2 SHIRAZ
South Australia

Extravagantly rich and powerful, and densely fruited, the dark wines made from the Shiraz grape variety are characterized by a natural exuberance and warmth.

Buying advice Australian Shiraz comes in many forms. The classic style comes from Barossa and McLaren Vale in South Australia; for spicier versions look to Heathcote and the Grampians in Victoria.

Food pairing Barbecued meat, rich stews.

Also try Zinfandel from the USA; Shiraz from South Africa.

Ripe, organic Malbec grapes *growing in the vineyard of the Familia Zuccardi Bodega in Mendoza, Argentina.*

3 PINOT NOIR
New Zealand

Supple, succulent, and silky wines from the Pinot Noir grape variety have an extra dimension of purity, if slightly less savoury complexity, than the same grape produced in Burgundy.

Buying advice Regions to look for include Central Otago, Marlborough, and Martinborough
Food pairing Lamb, duck, salmon, tuna.
Also try Pinot Noirs from Oregon, Chile's Leyda Valley, and Tasmania and Victoria in Australia.

4 MALBEC
Argentina

Made from vines grown at high altitudes, the Malbec grape variety produces vivaciously fruited and fresh but powerful reds with a beguiling aromatic intensity.

Buying advice Mendoza is the primary region for Malbec, but look out for Patagonia and Salta.
Food pairing Char-grilled steak.
Also try Compare with the Malbec of Cahors, France; South African Cabernet Franc, and Tannat from Uruguay and Argentina.

Explore

Sparkling Wines of the World

Sparkling wines are made all over the world,
and in all colours. In this tasting we will be
looking at four of the most popular styles –
and they are not all called Champagne.

Vineyards in Aÿ-Champagne, France.

As we saw on p.16 and p.35, sparkling wine is produced by first producing a still wine and then turning it fizzy with carbon dioxide bubbles – by injecting them in a process of carbonation (like a fizzy soft drink), or by adding yeast and sugar for a secondary fermentation in bottles or tanks. Only the wines made with a secondary fermentation in bottle (the *méthode champenoise*) in the Champagne region of northeast France are genuine Champagne. Spanish winemakers also use this method to create Cava, as do the Germans for Sekt and South Africans for Cap Classique. It is also used to make the best sparkling wines in Australia, the USA, and southern England. For Prosecco, the Italians carry out secondary fermentation in tanks, a process known as Charmat.

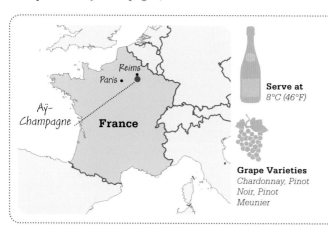

Reims
Paris •
Aÿ-
Champagne   **France**

Serve at
8°C (46°F)

Grape Varieties
Chardonnay, Pinot
Noir, Pinot
Meunier

1 CHAMPAGNE
France

The cool Champagne region of northern France is widely considered to produce the best sparkling wines in the world, made from one or all of Pinot Noir, Pinot Meunier, and Chardonnay grapes.

Look for Gosset Brut Excellence; Delamotte Brut NV

Tasting Session

2 PROSECCO
Italy

Lighter, softer wines produced with the Charmat method in the Prosecco zone north of Venice and Treviso, in northeast Italy, have become hugely popular in the past decade.

Look for Bisol Cartizze Prosecco di Valdobbiadene; Adami Bosco di Gica Prosecco di Valdobbiadene

Serve at
8°C (46°F)

Grape Variety
Glera

3 CAVA
Spain

Mostly produced in Catalonia in eastern Spain, but also permitted in a number of other Spanish regions, Cava is made with the traditional method, usually from a blend of three local grape varieties.

Look for Agustí Torelló Mata Brut Reserva; Albet i Noya Petit Albet

Serve at
8°C (46°F)

Grape Varieties
Macabeo, Parellada, Xarel-lo, Chardonnay, Pinot Noir

4 ENGLISH SPARKLING
England

At the northern limit of wine producing climates, southeast England can make high-quality sparkling wines using the same grape varieties and methods as Champagne.

Look for Nyetimber Classic Cuvée; Ridgeview Bloomsbury Cuvée Merret

Serve at
8°C (46°F)

Grape Varieties
Chardonnay, Pinot Noir, Pinot Meunier

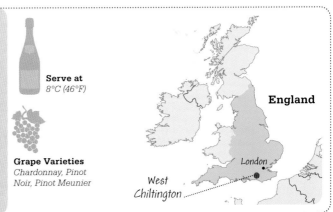

1 CHAMPAGNE
France

"Brut" means a dryer style of Champagne

Appearance Lemon yellow to gold. Fine persistent bubbles snaking from the bottom-centre to the top of the glass, forming a ring as they move to the edge.

A sign of quality, this cheminée *(chimney) effect is caused by a carefully managed second fermentation in the bottle.*

Aroma Gently insistent apples and citrus fruit, with pastry and biscuits.

Complex pastry notes come from contact with dead yeast cells or lees in the bottle after second fermentation.

Flavour Crisp lemon and apple with a kind of steely and mineral purity. Toasty finish.

Champagne grapes are grown on chalky soils in northeastern France where the climate is cool and grapes are harvested with a high degree of acidity for that mouth-cleaning, mineral sensation.

Texture Soft, delicate, long-lasting bubbles. Creamy.

The contact with the lees gives extra body and a buttery feeling in the mouth, offset by subtle bubbles and that cleansing acidity.

"Exhilaratingly crisp yet complex fizz from the Champagne region."

2 PROSECCO
Italy

.....The company seal of Bisol, a top Prosecco producer

 Appearance Pale yellow with green tints. Frothy mousse of large bubbles that dissipates quite quickly.

Prosecco has its secondary fermentation in a tank, which yields slightly larger, more short-lived bubbles than in bottle-fermented sparkling wines.

 Aroma Light delicate notes of pear and white flowers.

The white Glera grape variety (which used to be called Prosecco) is less strongly flavoured than the Champagne trio.

 Flavour Icing sugar, lemons, and pears.

Prosecco tends to be a little sweeter than most sparkling wines, a result of the sugar added before bottling. The sweetness combines with the bubbles to give a foaming, icing sugar-like sensation.

 Texture Light-bodied and graceful, almost weightless.

Prosecco feels lighter than Champagne because it does not have the lees contact to give it extra body. The best have a gossamer freshness that makes them a great apéritif.

"Light and easy to drink with subtle floral and pear flavours."

3 CAVA
Spain

Cava uses the same terms as Champagne to indicate style, such as Brut for dry ....

BRUT

VINIFICAT A • • LA PROPIETAT

AGUSTÍ TORELLÓ MATA
R E S E R V A

· C · A · V · A ·

SANT SADURNÍ D'ANOIA (BARCELONA) ESPAÑA

Appearance Straw-yellow with a touch of green. Fine bead of mousse.

The best Cavas are made using the same techniques as Champagne and have equally fine bubbles in the same "chimney" effect (see p.132).

Aroma Intense ripe apples, pineapple, and a slight earthy edge.

Cava varies in quality and intensity. In the better quality versions, labelled as Gran Reserva, the fruit flavours are more marked and the earthy character less pronounced.

Flavour Rich and earthy with ripe apples and the pleasingly sour tang of grapefruit.

The fruit flavours of Cava's traditional grape varieties Macabeo, Parellada, and Xarel-lo (which imparts the earthy flavours), mixed sometimes with Chardonnay and Pinot Noir.

Texture Dry and quite dense on the palate.

Cava is made in a much warmer climate than Champagne, leading to grapes with much less obvious acidity. It is usually dry but, like Champagne, it will have varying degrees of sugar added before final bottling.

"Rich Spanish take on traditional-method sparkling wine."

4 ENGLISH SPARKLING
England

Appearance Lemon-yellow to pale gold. Fine persistent bubbles snake from the bottom-centre to the top of the glass, forming a ring as they move to the edge.

The best English sparkling wine looks very similar to Champagne. It is made in the same way, usually from the same grape varieties grown on similar (chalky) soils.

Aroma Clean red apple, a touch floral with hedgerow hawthorn character, lemon. Some toasty and biscuit notes.

The distinctive floral-and-green character is more apparent in wines that contain the Seyval Blanc grape variety.

Flavour Crisp and fresh, bright red apple, and pastry-brioche notes.

Like the best Champagnes, the best English sparkling wines enjoy long periods of fermenting in the bottle, for those baker's shop flavours.

Texture Feels bright and mouthwatering.

English wine has very high natural acidity, being produced in very cool climates at the northern limits of wine production.

Nyetimber was one of the first English producers to capture world attention

"Searingly crisp with wild hedgerow aromas."

Choosing Your Wine

Sparkling wine is made all over the world. Winemakers get the bubbles by first making a still wine and then giving it a second fermentation or adding carbon dioxide. Sparkling wine works best when the grapes have plenty of acidity (when they are grown in a cooler climate and harvested early). It's a classic aperitif, but it also works well with certain food.

Champagne Deutz has been produced since the 19th century, a time of huge growth for Champagne.

1 CHAMPAGNE
France

The original sparkling wine and still widely regarded as the best, Champagne, from the region of the same name in northeast France, is characterized by its unique balance of richness and fine, cleansing freshness.

Buying advice Most Champagne is a blend of wines from different vintages (marked NV). For the finest expressions of the best single vintages, look for labels marked Vintage.
Food pairing Champagne tastes wonderful with fish and seafood such as smoked salmon.
Also try Wines made using the same method (known as *méthode champenoise*) from Tasmania (Australia), New Zealand, and northern California in the USA.

2 PROSECCO
Italy

This light, elegant, gentle sparkling wine is made using the tank (Charmat) method in northeast Italy. It is produced from the Glera grape variety and has a pear, lemon, and icing sugar character.

Buying advice The best quality examples come from the Prosecco di Conegliano de Valdobbiadene DOCG.
Food pairing Prosecco is the perfect apéritif, but it also works well with many lightly sweet fruit desserts.
Also try Aromatic Italian sparkling wines Asti Spumante and Moscato d'Asti or the Champagne-like Franciacorta.

3 CAVA
Spain

Predominantly produced from grapes grown in the Catalan region, Cava uses three local varieties to make sparkling wine by the traditional bottle-fermented method. Occasional additions of Champagne and Pinot Noir can also be used to create a richer, earthier fizz.

Buying advice Look at the labels on Cava bottles for an indication of the flavour – wines marked Gran Reserva will be older and will tend to have a richer style.

One of the largest *producers of Champagne, Mumm also makes similar wines in California.*

Food pairing Seafood and salads, or as an apéritif.

Also try Crémant or Blanquette de Limoux from the Languedoc across the border in the French Pyrenees.

4 ENGLISH SPARKLING
England

England's cool climate and soils have proved to be surprisingly ideal for sparkling wine production. English winemakers use the same techniques and grape varieties as Champagne with the resulting examples characterized by a slightly more floral style.

Buying advice Since the English sparkling wine industry is still small (despite a relatively long tradition of winemaking), you may need to shop around to actually find a bottle, and even then choices may be limited.

Food pairing English sparkling wine works well with fish and seafood, or as an apéritif.

Also try Sparkling wines from Germany known as Sekt; Crémant de Bourgogne and Crémant de Loire from France.

Once the preserve *of nobility, these days sparkling wine is widely used as a celebratory drink.*

3

Take it further

Raise your knowledge and understanding of wine to the next level by exploring some of the key factors that determine its style and taste profile. Is the wine from a cool or a warm climate? Has the winemaker used oak barrels? How long should you keep a bottle of wine? And what food could you drink it with?

In this section, learn about:

The Effect of Oak
pp.140–147

The Effect of Climate
pp.148–155

The Effect of Age
pp.156–163

Something Completely Different
pp.164–175

How to Match Wine and Food
pp.176–187

Explore

The Effect of Oak

The use of oak barrels in winemaking can have a profound effect on the finished wine. Even the type of oak barrel can influence the flavour of the wine, thereby making oak one of the key parts of a winemaker's toolkit.

Oak barrels *in a South American winery.*

Historically, most wine was made in oak or other wooden barrels. Today most wines are fermented in stainless steel or concrete vats, which impart no flavour. Some wines are bottled immediately, others are transferred to oak barrels to age for months or years. Oak lends flavours of toast, vanilla, and coconut – to what degree depends on where the wood was grown, how the barrel was made, how large, and how old it is. New barrels add more flavour than old. American oak tends to lend more coconut and vanilla than French oak. The longer a wine spends in oak, the greater the effect. Another variable is the degree of "toasting". When a barrel is made, its insides are heated or toasted to release aromatic compounds, and barrels come with light, medium, or heavy toast.

South Island, New Zealand

Blenheim

Wellington

Christchurch

Serve at
8°C (46°F)

Grape Variety
Sauvignon Blanc

1 UNOAKED WHITE
New Zealand Sauvignon Blanc

In New Zealand most Sauvignon Blanc is fermented and aged in stainless steel vats at cold temperatures, to keep the delicate, aromatic fruit flavours.

Look for Cloudy Bay or Seresin Estate Sauvignon Blanc

Tasting Session

2 OAKED WHITE
Barrel-fermented New Zealand Sauvignon Blanc
This uses the same grape variety, but is fermented and aged in small French oak barrels for a different texture and more complex flavours.

Look for Cloudy Bay Te Koko Sauvignon Blanc; Seresin Marama Sauvignon Blanc

Serve at
10–12°C
(50–54°F)

Grape Variety
Sauvignon Blanc

South Island, New Zealand

Blenheim

Wellington

Christchurch

Argentina

Mendoza

Lujan de Cuyo

Buenos Aires

Serve at
14°C (57°F)

Grape Variety
Malbec

3 UNOAKED RED
Argentinian Malbec
Using the Malbec variety grown in Argentina's high-altitude vineyards and made in stainless steel or cement vats, unoaked Malbec is designed to be more exuberantly fruity than the barrel-aged version.

Look for Viñalba Malbec; Colomé Terruno Malbec

4 OAKED RED
Barrel-matured Argentinian Malbec
Most Argentinian Malbec is given some time with oak, either by ageing in barrels or by adding cheaper oak chips or staves to the stainless steel or concrete vats.

Look for Viñalba Gran Reserva Malbec; Colomé Estate Malbec

Serve at
16–18°C
(60–64°F)

Grape Variety
Malbec

Argentina

Mendoza

Lujan de Cuyo

Buenos Aires

1 UNOAKED WHITE
New Zealand Sauvignon Blanc

 Appearance Bright, pale straw-yellow with green tinge.

An unoaked white wine will generally have a paler colour than a wine made from the same grape variety in new oak barrels.

 Aroma Vivacious, bright, pungent, green aromas of gooseberry and grass; elderflower and passion fruit.

Sauvignon Blanc is a naturally exuberant grape variety – winemakers try to keep the grapes and juice as cool as possible, from vineyard to bottle, to preserve those flavours.

 Flavour Zesty citrus fruit with gooseberry, passion fruit, and elderflower cordial.

Unoaked white wines are all about pure, if quite simple, fruit flavours. Winemakers use specific types of yeast to accentuate these flavours.

 Texture Light, crisp, fresh – the wine feels vivacious and lively on the palate.

An unoaked white will have less weight on the palate than those that are fermented and aged in oak barrels.

CLOUDY BAY

SAUVIGNON BLANC 2011

Cloudy Bay was one of the first New Zealand producers to enjoy success with Sauvignon Blanc

"Crisp, light, aromatic, and fruity."

New Zealand wines are almost always closed with a screwcap to preserve freshness

2 OAKED WHITE
Barrel-fermented
New Zealand Sauvignon Blanc

Appearance Deeper and with more of a golden hue.

The chemistry of what happens to white wines in barrels is complex, but the richer colour is thought to be the result of the wine reacting with oxygen, which enters in small but constant quantities through the oak.

Aroma Intense. Peaches, nuts, honeysuckle, and a hint of smokiness.

Smokiness and nuts are classic flavours of barrel-fermented white wines.

Flavour Rich tropical fruit and lemon tart, with a nutty finish. Complex.

Making wines in barrel requires care: too much time in oak, poor-quality barrels, or low-quality fruit will lead to the fruit flavours being overwhelmed by oaky flavours.

Texture Mellow and full-bodied. Opulent and long.

The slow but constant interaction with oxygen and the stirring of the dead yeast cells or lees result in a wine with more weight and a richer texture.

"Rich and opulent, weighty and complex."

3 UNOAKED RED
Argentinian Malbec

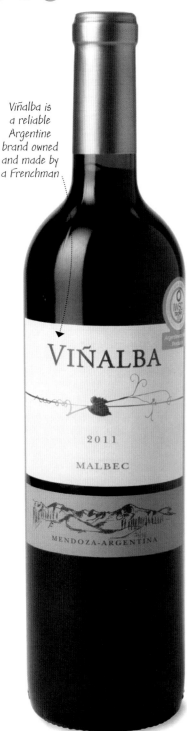

Viñalba is a reliable Argentine brand owned and made by a Frenchman

Appearance Vibrant purple-ruby with violet tints.

Unoaked reds are generally sold and drunk young, and made with little contact with oxygen, which would bring garnet and brick-like colours.

Aroma Extremely bright and full of fresh fruit: plum, black cherry, violets.

As with the unoaked white, this red is made in flavour-neutral stainless steel to bring the bright fruity aromas to the fore.

Flavour Vivacious black fruit with a twist of black chocolate.

As oak barrels are expensive, unoaked reds tend to be cheaper, but that doesn't mean less flavour. The best have intense fruit that shows off the character of the grape variety.

Texture Juicy, succulent, lively, and fresh.

Unoaked red wines are usually much less tannic than oaked red wines: winemakers are careful to extract less tannin from the skins and pips because they will not undergo the softening that comes from oak ageing.

"Supple, succulent, and fresh red wines with pure fruit flavours."

4 OAKED RED
Argentinian Malbec Reserva or Gran Reserva

The sticker shows this wine has won an award for quality in a wine competition

Appearance Dark, dense purple-ruby with violet tints fading to a very subtle brick-like colour on the rim.

Oaked wines have much more contact with oxygen, which enters the wine through the surface of the oak. Wines that have spent a long time in barrel have a tawny colour.

Aroma Plum and black cherry, coffee, vanilla, toast.

The coffee, toast, and vanilla aromas are all directly imparted by the barrel. As the wine ages, these aromas integrate with the fruit, forming a complex harmonious "bouquet".

Flavour Mocha, with dark chocolate-covered cherries.

Grape varieties that produce dark and powerful wines cope better with new and heavily toasted oak than lighter grape varieties, whose flavours can be submerged.

Texture Full-bodied, rich with soft tannins.

Winemakers like oak for its textural impact. The subtle interaction with small quantities of oxygen helps soften the tannins.

"Rich and complex with a powerful yet also well-rounded texture."

Choosing Your Wine

The traditional vessel for fermenting wine, the oak barrel has stood the test of time, allowing wines to age gracefully thanks to the slow absorption of oxygen. However, not all wine styles work well with oak, and winemakers must choose the make, degree of toasting, age, and size of barrel with care to suit their requirements.

1 UNOAKED WHITE
New Zealand Sauvignon Blanc
Made in stainless steel fermentation tanks, this young wine has exuberant gooseberry, grass, and tropical fruit aromas and flavours with a light, fresh, crisp feel.

Buying advice Almost all New Zealand Sauvignon Blanc is made in this style, but check the back label for the winemaker's notes.
Food pairing Fish, seafood, and mildly spicy Asian food.
Also try Unoaked whites such as Albariño from Spain and Sauvignon Blanc and Riesling from all over the world.

2 OAKED WHITE
Barrel-fermented New Zealand Sauvignon Blanc
Fermenting and ageing in barrel brings, in this case at least, a richer, denser texture and complex flavours of honeysuckle, stone fruit, lemon tart, nuts, and toast.

Buying advice The price of the barrels themselves, as well as the more time- and labour-intensive wine production process, is reflected in the higher price of barrel-fermented/oak-aged white wines.
Food pairing Chicken, pork, and other white meats.
Also try Barrel-fermented Sauvignon/Sémillon blends from the Graves region of Bordeaux; or any oak-aged Chardonnay produced all around the world.

The oak-ageing process can lead to richer, denser flavours and textures in the wine.

Some wines can be stored *in barrels for many years, but others do not benefit from oak-ageing and should be drunk while young.*

3 UNOAKED RED
Argentinian Malbec

Wonderfully vivacious black cherry and plum fruit flavours are very much to the fore in an unoaked Malbec, as the wine simply showcases the pure fruit flavours of the grape variety, without any other influences.

Buying advice Whether a red is unoaked or not is rarely indicated on the label, so you may have to check its origins with your trusted wine merchant.

Food pairing Sausages and charcuterie.

Also try Wines that often have little or no oak influence include Beaujolais from France, cheaper Spanish reds (sometimes marked "Joven", meaning "young"), and Dolcetto from Italy.

4 OAKED RED
Barrel-matured Argentinian Malbec

Powerfully textured and dense but with great softness and generosity, oak-aged Argentinian Malbec adds notes of mocha-coffee, toast, and vanilla to the black cherry and plum fruit found in the unoaked version.

Buying advice In Spain the Reserva or Gran Reserva categories have strict legal requirements; this is not the case in Argentina, but the presence of either term on the label usually indicates a certain degree of oak ageing.

Food pairing Grilled or barbecued steak and other red meat.

Also try Cabernet Sauvignon from around the world; for wines with long oak ageing, Rioja Gran Reserva.

Explore

The Effect of Climate

The specific climate in the region where the grapes are grown has a huge influence in determining a finished wine's aroma, flavour, and texture.

Winemakers are looking for that point when the grape has the ideal balance between sugars, acidity, and physiological ripeness (when the skin and pips have turned from green to brown, and the compounds that will create flavours during winemaking have developed). Factors such as soil, grape variety, and growing techniques play an important role, but generally speaking the warmer the climate, the higher the sugar and the lower the level of acidity will be once a grape has reached physiological ripeness. Thus warmer climates tend to produce richer, denser wines that are higher in alcohol and lower in acidity; cooler climates make lighter wines with lower alcohol and a crisper, fresher feeling from the higher acidity.

The Sonoma region *in northern California is warm and sunny.*

Vinho Verde

Porto

Lisbon

Portugal

Serve at
8°C (46°F)

Grape Variety
Loureiro, Trajadura, Alvarinho

1 COOL-CLIMATE WHITE
Vinho Verde
Cooled by the Atlantic Ocean, the Vinho Verde region in northwest Portugal produces fresh whites that can be dry or off-dry, and which sometimes have a little spritz of fine bubbles.

Look for Afros Vinho Verde; Quinta de Azevedo

Tasting Session

2 WARM-CLIMATE WHITE
Languedoc Viognier
The Viognier grape works well in the Languedoc region in the south of France, where the warm Mediterranean climate allows the grapes to develop their full range of flavours and rich texture.

Look for La Forge Viognier; Laurent Miquel Viognier

Serve at
12°C (54°F)

Grape Variety
Viognier

3 COOL-CLIMATE RED
Loire Valley Cabernet Franc
The cool, northerly Loire Valley is best known for its white wines, but the early-ripening Cabernet Franc also produces succulent reds.

Look for Cave de Vignerons de Saumur Cabernet Franc; Domaine Filliatreau Saumur-Champigny

Serve at
13°C (55°F)

Grape Variety
Cabernet Franc

4 WARM-CLIMATE RED
Californian Zinfandel
A Californian speciality, Zinfandel thrives in the warmer parts of California, producing wines that are high in alcohol with very concentrated ripe berry fruit.

Look for Ravenswood Lodi Zinfandel; Joseph Swan Vineyards Mancini Ranch Zinfandel

Serve at
18°C (64°F)

Grape Variety
Zinfandel

1 COOL-CLIMATE WHITE
Vinho Verde

Quality-minded producer
Afros has helped revitalize
the image of Vinho Verde

Appearance Pale silver-green.

As we have seen throughout the book, pale colour in a wine is a good indication that it comes from a cooler climate.

Aroma Delicate floral notes with pear, green apples, and subtle citrus.

Cooler climate whites will generally err more towards the citrus and orchard fruit end of the spectrum, rather than tropical.

Flavour Very fresh, almost bracing, lemon and lime fruit, crunchy green apples, a touch of peach.

The higher acidity in this wine gives it a distinctively fresh feel. Vinho Verde that uses Alvarinho has a more peachy character.

Texture Very light with a slight prickle and spritz of bubbles.

This light fizz is a tradition in Vinho Verde, which today is usually the result of the addition of carbon dioxide before the wine is bottled. All cool-climate whites have low alcohol, but Vinho Verde is especially low at 11% or less.

"Mouthwateringly fresh citrus and apples."

2 WARM-CLIMATE WHITE
Languedoc Viognier

Appearance Bright straw-yellow to gold.

The Viognier grape skins are yellow when they reach ripeness, leading to wines with a golden colour.

Aroma Intense. Abundant peaches, apricots, and honeysuckle; a touch of pineapple.

The classic nose of Viognier at full ripeness. In cooler climates, the nose is more muted with green notes.

Flavour Ripe and rich. Luscious, fleshy peaches and apricots.

Viognier needs a warm climate to ripen because it has thick skins, which provide plenty of flavour, but which can be bitter when harvested too soon.

Texture Very weighty and full in the mouth. Long, powerful.

Viognier attains a high level of sugar by the time its skins and pips have ripened, leading to more alcohol and a more ample feeling in the mouth. Viognier is never high in acidity, but growers must be careful to harvest before the acidity gets too low, making for a flabby, lifeless wine.

La Forge is a brand name of prolific Languedoc producer Domaines Paul Mas

"Luscious peaches and a golden hue."

3 COOL-CLIMATE RED
Loire Valley Cabernet Franc

 Appearance Bright ruby-red with purple hints.

Cabernet Franc is related to Cabernet Sauvignon, but has thinner skins with less pigment, ripening earlier, which makes it suitable for cooler climates.

 Aroma Perfumed – violets and fruits of the forest. Some leafy, herbaceous aromas.

Cool-climate reds tend to have a more gentle aromatic quality – think back to the Pinot Noirs (see pp.85 and 106) and other light, elegant, and fresh fruity wines we've tasted in this course. The same grape grown in warmer climates tends to become jammier in character.

 Flavour Some graphite or pencil lead along with the forest fruits and touches of green.

In cool vintages, growers struggle to ripen Cabernet Franc and the green flavours take over. In warmer vintages, those green notes provides an attractive seasoning.

 Texture Crunchy, succulent, with a little gripping sensation.

Cabernet Franc has less tannin than Cabernet Sauvignon, but those tannins need to ripen. In very cool vintages, the wines can be uncomfortably astringent.

This wine is produced by a co-operative of growers throughout the Saumur region

"Succulent, aromatic, and freshly fruity."

4 WARM-CLIMATE RED
Californian Zinfandel

 Appearance The best examples are a dark and dense ruby-red.

Warm-climate reds will usually have a much denser colour than cool-climate reds, although the amount of time the winemaker decides to leave the skins in touch with the juice is a more important factor.

 Aroma A real explosion of sweet fruit with very ripe blueberries and plums.

The fruit character of warm climate wines will generally tend towards darker, less delicately aromatic fruit characters.

 Flavour Powerful fruitiness as with the aroma, the fruit may shade into raisins or prunes.

Timing the picking of Zinfandel is a tricky business: it needs plenty of time to ripen, but it can quickly take up an unattractive raisined, stewed, or baked character if left too long.

Texture Dense and warm and supple. Big but soft.

Zinfandel grapes accumulate a lot of sugar by the time they ripen; this leads to high alcohol wines – some of the world's biggest, regularly in excess of 15%.

Ravenswood produces powerful Zinfandels and has the motto, "No wimpy wines!"

 "Big, sweetly fruited, and strong."

Choosing Your Wine

Climate is not the same as weather: the former refers to the long-term meteorological character of a region, while the latter is the day-to-day circumstances. Climate can vary even within a small region depending on factors such as altitude and proximity to ocean, forests, or rivers. So while climate information on the label is a useful guide to the style of wine, it is not always 100% accurate. For example, a wine from a generally cool climate may have a different character in a warmer year.

1 COOL-CLIMATE WHITE
Vinho Verde

A classic style from northern Portugal, Vinho Verde (literally translated as "green wine", but meaning "young wine") is lemon-fresh, slightly spritzy, and low in alcohol.

Buying advice Vinho Verde is seldom expensive, but it's usually best to avoid the very cheapest examples as they can taste synthetically sweet and acidic.

Food pairing Seafood; Portuguese salted cod (known locally as *bacalhau*).

Also try Other cool-climate whites from Chablis, Muscadet (France), Mosel (Germany), Rías Baixas (Spain), Carneros (California), and the South Island of New Zealand.

2 WARM-CLIMATE WHITE
Languedoc Viognier

This forcefully aromatic golden-hued wine from the Viognier grape variety is made in the warm climate of southern France, close to the Mediterranean Sea.

Buying advice Viognier is best drunk young while it is still at its most aromatically exuberant.

Food pairing White meats in rich sauces; Chinese food.

Also try Viognier from the Rhône Valley (France), Australia, and California; as well as wines made from Marsanne and Roussanne grape varieties.

Many traditional *French vineyards have grown up around a large house or château.*

California, USA *has the perfect conditions for growing warm-climate wines and boasts many vineyards such as this Clos du Bois winery in Sonoma County.*

3 COOL-CLIMATE RED
Loire Valley Cabernet Franc

With a texture reminiscent of crunchy just-ripe berries, and subtle floral edge to its aroma, Cabernet Franc is a highly refreshing, lightly coloured red wine produced in the cooler northerly part of France.

Buying advice Look for the Buorgueil, Chinon, and Saumur-Champigny appellations on the label for the best-quality examples of Cabernet Franc wines.

Food pairing Chicken, mild game, charcuterie, and meaty fish such as salmon and tuna all complement this style.

Also try Fresh, fruity reds such as Beaujolais, from France; and Dolcetto and Valpolicella from Italy.

4 WARM-CLIMATE RED
Californian Zinfandel

With intense blueberry and kola nut fruit, sometimes also combined with a touch of raisin or prune, there is an abundance of strong fruit flavour as well as lots of alcohol in this uniquely Californian warm-climate wine style.

Buying advice Styles of Zinfandel vary dramatically, from the brightly juicy-fruity to the big and powerful – it is often best to consult your retailer before you buy.

Food pairing For powerful styles go for barbecued and roasted meat and hearty meat stews; for the juicy-fruity styles try charcuterie and salami.

Also try Fruity, powerful reds such as Plavac Mali in Croatia and Primitivo in Southern Italy.

Explore

The Effect of Age

One of the qualities that distinguishes wine from almost all other drinks is its ability to change and improve once it has been bottled. However, not all wines improve and those that do have the capacity to age need to be stored carefully.

Many wines are given a period of ageing, in a wooden barrel or in a stainless steel or cement tank, before they are bottled. After a few months in bottle, most do not improve – quite the reverse. A handful (maybe five per cent) age well, taking on more complex flavours and softening in texture, for years or even decades in bottle. The wine interacts with oxygen in a complex chemical process still not fully understood, but the higher the wine's tannin and acidity, the longer it will take to reach maturity. To be worth cellaring, a wine must also have sufficient levels of flavour compounds. To age satisfyingly, the wine must be stored in the dark at a consistent temperature (about 15°C / 59°F), with the bottle in a horizontal position to stop the cork drying out and breaking.

Casa Lapostolle wine cellar, Santa Cruz, Chile.

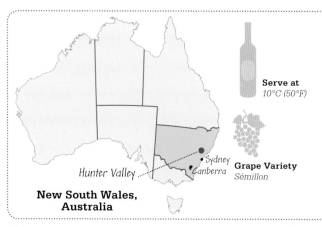

Serve at
10°C (50°F)

Grape Variety
Sémillon

Hunter Valley ···· *Sydney* *Canberra*

**New South Wales,
Australia**

**1 YOUNG WHITE
Young Hunter Valley
Sémillon**

A unique white wine style made from Sémillon in the Hunter Valley in New South Wales, Australia.

Look for Tyrrell's Hunter Valley Sémillon Vat 1; McWilliam's Mount Pleasant Lovedale Sémillon (2–3 years after the vintage on the label)

Tasting Session

2 AGED WHITE
Aged Hunter Valley Sémillon

Hunter Valley Sémillon ages well, taking on intriguing flavours for a decade or more in some cases.

Look for Tyrrell's Hunter Valley Sémillon Vat 1; McWilliam's Mount Pleasant Lovedale Sémillon (10+ years after the vintage on the label)

Serve at
10–12°C
(50–54°F)

Grape Variety
Sémillon

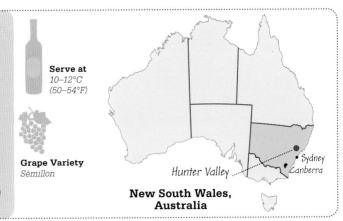

Hunter Valley .... • Sydney
• Canberra

New South Wales, Australia

• Paris

Saint-
Seurin-de-
Cadourne .... **France**

• Bordeaux

Serve at
16°C (61°F)

Grape Varieties
Cabernet Sauvignon, Merlot, Cabernet Franc, Petit Verdot

3 YOUNG RED
Young Bordeaux

Arguably the world's most famous, and certainly most imitated, red wine style, red Bordeaux is also sometimes called claret.

Look for Château Sociando-Mallet Haut-Médoc; Château Chasse-Spleen Moulis (2–3 years after the vintage on the label)

4 AGED RED
Aged Bordeaux

Because Bordeaux reds are so good at improving with time in the right conditions, they attract the interest of wine collectors the world over.

Look for Château Sociando-Mallet Haut-Médoc; Château Chasse-Spleen Moulis (10+ years after the vintage on the label)

Serve at
16–18°C
(61–64°F)

Grape Varieties
Cabernet Sauvignon, Merlot, Cabernet Franc, Petit Verdot

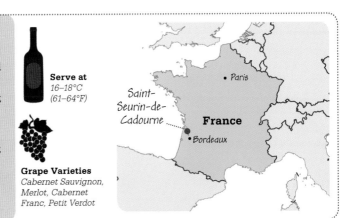

• Paris

Saint-
Seurin-de-
Cadourne .... **France**

• Bordeaux

1 YOUNG WHITE
Young Hunter Valley Sémillon

 Appearance Bright, pale, lemon-yellow with green tinges.

The sign of a young white wine is its brightness and absence of brown tinges. The slight green tinges are typical of the Sémillon grape variety.

 Aroma Not hugely aromatic. Some fresh lemon and lime and a little cut-grass or herbaceous edge.

Most Hunter Valley Sémillon is made in stainless steel tanks, so there are no oaky vanilla or butter flavours in the wine at this stage.

 Flavour Really vibrant, fresh, and dry, with racy lemon-and-lime citrus, crisp apple, and grass.

Those flavours indicate a high level of acidity in the wine; the Hunter Valley Sémillon harvest in New South Wales is generally much earlier than the rest of Australia.

 Texture Very light with a clean, long finish.

Because of that early harvest, Hunter Valley Sémillon grapes do not accumulate high sugars, and therefore alcohol, as in many other areas of Australia; the resulting wine is dry but with alcohol of 11%.

The young wine is bright and pale in the glass

"The bone-dry young white tastes of fresh citrus, apple, and grassiness, while the aged white is magnificently complex with a toasty-limey richness."

2 AGED WHITE
Aged Hunter Valley Sémillon

 Appearance A bright, deep gold that intensifies as the wine ages for more than a decade.

White wine begins to show these golden colours as it interacts over time with the small amount of oxygen present in the bottle.

 Aroma Still that citrus character, but more intensely limey. Also notes of toast and honey and lanolin or wet wool.

The complex interaction of the wine's chemical properties with oxygen brings about this curious combination of aromas.

Many Australian producers now use screwcaps rather than corks, to keep the wine fresher

 Flavour The lime has intensified but now it tastes more like lime on buttered toast drizzled with honey.

Hunter Valley Sémillon goes through many phases as it ages: from bright, fresh, and dry in youth, through a brief one-to-two year period where the flavours and aromas are muted, to this rich, toasty style, which begins to develop after five years.

 Texture Still quite light and fresh, but harmonious and concentrated.

High acidity in white wines is thought to be a key factor in letting it age. Wines that go through malolactic conversion (turning harsher malic acid to softer lactic acid during the winemaking process) do not usually age as well.

TYRRELL'S WINES

*Vat 1
Hunter Semillon*

1999

The wine takes on a more golden hue as it ages

3 YOUNG RED
Young Bordeaux

 Appearance Bright purple-ruby, quite dense.

As we have seen on p.107, Bordeaux is made from blends of grape varieties including thick-skinned Cabernet Sauvignon and Petit Verdot, which give a dark colour to the wines in their youth.

 Aroma Quite simple but intense. Bright blackcurrant; some toast, coffee, and vanilla.

Young red wines are dominated by simple fruit aromas. Red Bordeaux are aged in new oak barrels, imparting toast, coffee, and vanilla aromas.

 Flavour As with the aroma, it is the highly concentrated blackcurrant fruit and toasty oak that dominate.

These are the classic flavours of young Bordeaux blends. The fruit flavours feel very intense at this stage – some people like this, others prefer to let the flavours settle down and mellow.

 Texture Quite astringent and dry – a grainy texture.

Red Bordeaux is full of tannin and acidity when it is young. These, along with concentrated flavours, are the necessary ingredients if a wine is to age well.

The colour of young red wine is vibrant, almost purple

"The young red has notes of bright blackcurrant in an astringent package, while the aged red is harmonious, smooth, long, and savoury."

4 AGED RED
Aged Bordeaux

Appearance A bright ruby core with a brick or tile-like rim. Some sediment.

In each bottle of red wine, complex interactions between oxygen and the compounds leached from the grape skins during winemaking change the colour and release a harmless sediment. Always allow older reds to stand for a few hours before drinking.

Aroma Very complex. The blackcurrant is now joined by cedar wood, leather, pencil lead, and earthy aromas.

A vast range of complex chemical changes occur as a red wine ages, each contributing a different set of aromas. Leave the glass for a while and come back to it: in a quality wine, still more aromas will have been released.

If the wine is very old, take care when removing the cork – it may crumble

Flavour Harmonious but complex. Savoury as well as fruity.

Compared to the young red Bordeaux, the older wine will feel much less disjointed. In a good wine, the toasty flavours will feel much less evident; like a meat stew, the flavours will have evolved and "married".

Texture Smooth and elegant. Still bright, very easy to drink.

As a wine ages, the tannins soften and the acidity becomes less evident, making it feel smooth and silky. A fine aged wine will have a very long finish – you will still taste it long after you've swallowed.

Allow the wine to stand for a few hours before serving, to allow the harmless sediment to settle

Château
ciando-Mallet
HAUT - MÉDOC
1996
MIS EN BOUTEILLE AU CHATEAU

Choosing Your Wine

Wine is famous for its ability to age, but you must always remember that not all wines improve, and not everyone likes the taste of aged wine. If you're ageing the wine yourself, make sure that you have a consistently cool, dark storage place, and if you're buying old wine, make sure that you trust the vendor.

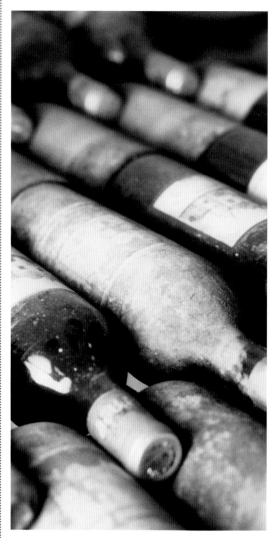

If you're ageing wine *at home, make sure that you know exactly how long it should age for.*

1 YOUNG WHITE
Young Hunter Valley Sémillon
In the first year or two after vintage, Hunter Valley Sémillon is pale in colour and tight and lean in texture, with a lemon-and-lime, grassy freshness.

Buying advice Look for top names such as Tyrrells, Mount Pleasant, and Brokenwood.
Food pairing At this stage of its evolution, it works best with seafood.
Also try Compare and contrast with Sémillon-Sauvignon Blanc blends from Bordeaux and Western Australia's Margaret River region.

2 AGED WHITE
Aged Hunter Valley Sémillon
After ten years in the bottle, the flavours of Hunter Valley Sémillon intensify and change, taking on flavours of honey, toast, and lanolin while maintaining their limey freshness. The best continue to improve.

Buying advice It's fun to buy a case of six-to-twelve bottles, and drink one (or so) each year to see how it changes.
Food pairing The richer, toastier flavours work well with white meat such as roast chicken, or pork.
Also try Other long-lived white wines include Riesling, white Burgundy, and Chenin Blanc from the Loire and South Africa.

Grapes growing in a Bordeaux vineyard *in the St Émilion district, Aquitaine, France.*

3 YOUNG RED
Young Bordeaux red

Vivacious fruit aromas and obvious toasty-oak notes dominate youthful Bordeaux red wines, with the high tannin content and acidity giving them quite a tough, astringent texture.

Buying advice If you want to drink young Bordeaux, go for cheaper wines with less oak from appellations such as Bordeaux Supérieur.
Food pairing Roast or grilled red meat dishes complement the flavours of the wine.
Also try Compare the structure and texture of young Bordeaux with Cabernet Sauvignon-Merlot blends from California, Australia, and Chile.

4 AGED RED
Aged Bordeaux red

An aged Bordeaux has very complex, harmonious flavours that develop in the glass and leave a long finish after swallowing. The texture is meltingly soft but still bright and fresh.

Buying advice If you're buying a wine to keep, make sure you have the right conditions – a dark place with a consistent, cool temperature.
Food pairing Duck, game, and mushroom dishes all complement an older Bordeaux.
Also try Red wine regions with a track record for ageing include good-quality Rioja, Barolo, Burgundy, California, and Rhône Valley.

Explore

Something Completely Different

There are some wines that divide opinion.
Using traditional techniques that are not widely employed
elsewhere, they are extreme in flavour, either savoury
or sweet, and utterly different from the mainstream.

Wine styles apart

As we have seen throughout this course,
it is very hard to generalize about wine,
because it is a drink with such a wide range
of styles and production techniques.
Fashions, flavours, and winemaking
philosophies change from country to
country and region to region, and different
winemakers have different views on exactly
how wine should be made. However, even
in the wide world of wine, there are some
wine styles that stand apart from the rest.

Six unique taste experiences

In this taste test, we'll look at six of the
most unusual styles, each of which have
evolved in specific regions. Traditional
white Rioja from the northeastern Spanish
region of the same name is as far from
modern white wine styles as it is possible to
get. Amarone from northeast Italy and Pedro

Ximénez sherry from southern Spain both
use dried grapes but yield very different
taste results. Vin Jaune from the Jura region
in eastern France takes its name from its
yellow colour and has a yeasty-nutty flavour.
Makers of Greek Retsina add pine resin to
their wine to give it a distinctive flavour,
while sparkling Shiraz is a uniquely powerful
fizzy red wine from Australia.

Try anything once

These styles are certainly not for everybody.
Like foods such as blue cheese, liquorice, or
anchovies, these wines are something of an
acquired taste. Just give them a chance,
however, and you may find that you love
them. Or, equally likely, you may find that
you hate them. At the very least, though,
they should make you marvel at the
remarkable range of flavours that can be
extracted from a single fruit, the grape.

Dried grapes *can provide interesting styles
such as Amarone and Pedro Ximénez sherry.*

Tasting Session

1 TRADITIONAL WHITE RIOJA
Spain

Long barrel-ageing creates golden wines, known locally as Rioja Blanco, full of complex savoury flavours that can last for decades.

Look for López de Heredia Viña Tondonia Gran Reserva Rioja Blanco; Marqués de Murrieta Castillo Ygay Gran Reserva Rioja Blanco

Serve at
*12–14°C
(54–57°F)*

Grape Varieties
*Viura, Malvasia,
Garnacha Blanca*

2 VIN JAUNE
France

Complex, nutty "yellow" wines aged beneath a layer of yeast in oak barrels in the Jura region.

Look for Domaine Pignier Vin Jaune; Domaine Jacques Puffeney Vin Jaune

Serve at
*12–14°C
(54–57°F)*

Grape Variety
Savignin

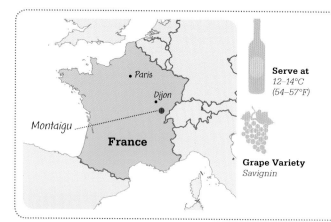

3 RETSINA
Greece

The addition of pine resin to the white grape juice during winemaking gives this Greek speciality its distinctive pine flavour and resinous texture.

Look for INO Retsina, Greece; Kourtaki Retsina

Serve at
*8–10°C
(46–50°F)*

Grape Varieties
*Savatiano, Assyrtiko,
Rhoditis*

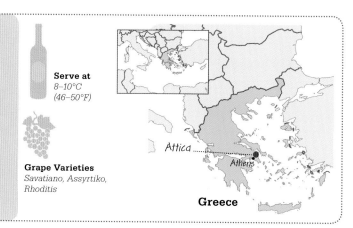

4 SPARKLING SHIRAZ
Australia

A classically full-bodied Australian red wine with bubbles, this is also a traditional Australian Christmas drink.

Look for Jacob's Creek Sparkling Shiraz; Majella Sparkling Shiraz

Serve at
*10–12°C
(50–54°F)*

Grape Variety
Shiraz

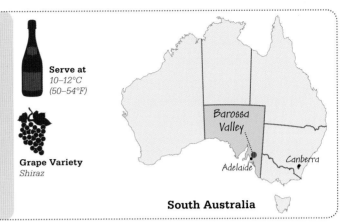

South Australia

Serve at
*16–18°C
(61–64°F)*

Grape Varieties
Corvina, Corvinone, Rondinella

5 AMARONE DELLA VALPOLICELLA
Italy

Made from red grapes that have been deliberately left to dry after harvest, Amarone is a powerful red with a bitter-sweet flavour.

Look for Allegrini Amarone della Valpolicella; Quintarelli Amarone della Valpolicella

6 PEDRO XIMÉNEZ SHERRY
Spain

Viscous, black, and sweet like treacle, Pedro Ximénez (widely referred to as PX) is a fortified wine from the Jerez region made from dried white grapes.

Look for Gonzalez Byass Noé PX Sherry; Osborne Venerable PX Sherry

Serve at
12°C (54°F)

Grape Variety
Pedro Ximénez

1 TRADITIONAL WHITE RIOJA
Spain

Appearance Deep golden colour with amber tints.

The colour indicates that this is an older white wine; traditional white Rioja from northeast Spain is released much later after vintage than most white wines.

Aroma Complex. Tobacco, honey, dried citrus fruit.

Traditional white Rioja can spend as many as six years in barrel. If the fruit is ripe and has good levels of acidity to begin with, it evolves complex flavours.

Flavour Rich honeyed and nutty flavours. Crystallized citrus fruit. Acacia.

Traditional white Riojas are prized for their "secondary" characters rather than their bright youthful fruit. Young wines made without oak from the same grape varieties are frequently neutral-tasting.

Texture Rich and long in finish – quite full-bodied, textured, but lively.

Grapes with good levels of acidity are vital to the texture of good white Rioja. Without it, the wines feel heavy and dull; with it, they are harmonious and rich.

"Nutty, complex, harmonious white wines."

...The badge of the Consejo Regulador de Rioja, which governs local wine production

Viña Tondonia is a brand of the Lopéz de Heredia winery

2 VIN JAUNE
France

Appearance Straw yellow to gold.

It's that colour that gives the wine its name – jaune means yellow in French.

Aroma Nutty and curry-like exotic spices. A touch of honey.

Made only in France's Jura region, Vin Jaune's unique winemaking process leads to high levels of a compound called sotolon, which has a distinctive fenugreek or turmeric-like aroma.

Flavour Nutty and curry-like exotic spices. A touch of honey.

Vin Jaune is aged in barrels beneath a naturally forming layer or "veil" of yeast, giving those nutty-yeasty flavours.

Texture Very dry. Full-bodied and long.

The aromas, flavours, and textures of Vin Jaune are similar to dry Fino sherry, but it is not fortified (no spirits have been added in the winemaking), and it is lower in alcohol (13% compared to 15% or more in sherry).

Vin Jaune
2001

dOMAI
PIGNI

Côtes du Jura

Vignerons à Montaigu

Vin Jaune is easy to spot thanks to its unique 62-cl bottles

"Curry spices, honey, and nuts in a long-lived, sherry-like dry wine."

3 RETSINA
Greece

Retsina takes its name from the Greek word for resin, rhetine

 Appearance Pale straw-yellow.

Most Retsina today is made from white grapes, although it is possible to find rosé versions.

 Aroma Lemon and lime with a strong, resinous whiff of pine needles.

Retsina gets its distinctive aromas from the winemaking process where small pieces of pine resin are added to the juice (known as "must") before fermentation.

 Flavour Fresh citrus with a subtle insinuation of pine.

The best versions of Retsina balance the pine resin with the crisp lemon flavours of the Saviatano and Assyrtiko grapes.

 Texture Feels slightly resinous – more viscous than other crisp, dry whites.

Modern Retsina-makers use much lower amounts of pine resin than in the past – but the process still give the wines a rounded, resinous feel.

"Pine resin and lemon – a taste of Greece."

Like Champagne, sparkling Shiraz is bottled with a cork at high pressure

4 SPARKLING SHIRAZ
Australia

Appearance Very dark purple with a foaming mousse of bubbles.

This style of red wine has been through a secondary, fizz-providing fermentation, either in the bottle or in a tank (see p.130).

Aroma Powerful blackberry and blueberry fruit with a touch of pepper and liquorice and a toasty edge.

Sparkling Shiraz is made from the same grape variety as still Australian Shiraz. It may also have some toasty-biscuity aromas from contact with dead yeast cells ("lees") in the bottle after the secondary fermentation.

Flavour Equally powerful as the nose, with a touch of chocolatey sweetness.

Winemakers add a dash of sweetening liquid to the wine after ageing before re-corking the bottle for release. Traditionally they use a sweet Port-style fortified wine.

Texture The tannin and density of a full-bodied red wine with the fine mousse of a sparkling white wine.

This combination is what makes sparkling Shiraz so unusual – it's rare to find full-bodied red wines with fizz.

ESTABLISHED 1847

JACOB'S CREEK

AUSTRALIA

Sparkling Shiraz

NAMED AFTER JACOB'S CREEK SITE
OF JOHANN GRAMP'S FIRST VINEYARD

CUVÉE

"An eccentric Australian classic."

The official seal of the Italian quality classification system ....

5 AMARONE DELLA VALPOLICELLA
Italy

Appearance Deep, dark purple-black.

Amarone is made from grapes that have been raisined (either on traditional wicker mats or in modern purpose-built drying rooms), so the ratio of skin to juice is high, making for a dark wine.

Aroma Lots of dark fruit, intense dark cherry, dried fruit, black chocolate.

Again the raisined character of the fruit used to make this wine comes through with those dried-fruit notes.

Flavour Extremely rich and complex. Dark chocolate-covered black cherries, and a slight twist of bitterness.

That bitter-sweet contrast is a distinctive feature of Amarone, a function of both the dried fruit used and the natural flavours of the Corvina grape variety.

Texture Densely textured and very rich. Strong but smooth, sometimes a little sweet.

The concentration of sugar in the grapes during the raisining process leads to alcohol as high as 17% in the finished wine. The grapes are sometimes so high in sugar that the yeast is unable to turn all of it into alcohol, leaving the finished wine slightly sweet.

"Intensely flavoured with bitter-sweet black cherries."

6 PEDRO XIMÉNEZ SHERRY
Spain

The average age of the wines blended to make this sherry is 30 years

Appearance Dense, opaque black-brown.

As with Amarone (and a handful of other wines around the world), Pedro Ximénez or PX sherry is made from grapes that have been left to dry in the sun after harvest.

Aroma Spicy fruitcake – very intense dried fruit (oranges, raisins), burnt toffee.

Pedro Ximénez is a white grape but the raisining process brings out "darker" flavours, which are accentuated by long ageing in oak barrels.

Flavour Treacle and concentrated dried-fruit syrup.

Made in a complex system of stacked barrels containing wines of different ages, known as a solera, all sherries are complex blends of wines of different ages or vintages.

Texture Very viscous and sweet – feels like dark syrup or treacle.

Like all sherries, PX is a fortified wine (see p.56). In PX, the winemaker adds the spirit when the wine still contains a lot of sugar, stopping the fermentation and leaving a sweet viscous wine.

"Treacly, very sweet but complex fruit cake-flavoured indulgence."

173

Choosing Your Wine

Many of the wines we've been tasting here have unique flavours and so they have very few direct equivalents. Moreover, they are often designed to complement local cuisines so don't always travel well outside their region of origin. However, they are well worth exploring on your wine journey as they will test the limits of your palate.

1 TRADITIONAL WHITE RIOJA
Spain

These long-lived and harmonious wines from the northeast of Spain are among the world's most complex white wines, featuring flavours of nuts, dried fruit, and even old furniture.

Buying advice The style of Rioja varies greatly, and it's not possible to tell from the label how it has been made. For this style look for respected producers such as Marqués de Murrieta or Lopéz de Heredia.

Food pairing Complementary foods include white meats, nuts, aged hard cheeses.

Also try Similarly complex nutty flavours can be found in some aged white Burgundies such as Meursault.

2 VIN JAUNE
France

From the Jura region of France, the Savignin grape variety is aged under a veil of yeast in oak barrels to produce extraordinary yellow wines with a character of honey and south Asian spice.

Buying advice Vin Jaune comes in a unique 62-cl bottle called a *clavelin*. Look for Château Chalon, Arbois, Côtes du Jura, and l'Etoile appellations.

Food pairing Aged Comté cheese; chicken with mushrooms.

Also try Fino and Manzanilla sherry from Spain are also aged under a layer of yeast and have many of the savoury flavours of Vin Jaune.

3 RETSINA
Greece

Fresh, lemony white (and occasionally rosé) wines with a resinous texture and notes of pine, the result of adding pine resin to the grape must (juice).

Buying advice High-quality Retsina can be hard to find outside Greece. Seek out a local Greek wine specialist, if you can.

Food pairing Greek meze such as marinated feta with olives or taramasalata.

Also try No wine is quite like Retsina. Try an elegant vermouth (an aromatic fortified wine) such as Chambèry, Noilly Prat, or Lillet from France, or Cinzano and Carpano from Italy.

4 SPARKLING SHIRAZ
Australia

A full-bodied red wine made from Shiraz grapes and transformed into a sparkling wine with a secondary fermentation, it is full of dark fruit, liquorice, and sometimes biscuit-like flavours.

Buying advice Sparkling Shiraz is designed to be consumed straightaway, but it can age, taking on complex leathery flavours like still Shiraz.

The many different styles of sherry *are all aged in oak barrels and produced in the region of Andalucía in Spain.*

Food pairing Hard cheeses, barbecues – in Australia it is often drunk with Christmas dinner.
Also try Lambrusco Rosso, a sparkling red wine from Italy, but take care to avoid the cheaper, supermarket brands.

5 AMARONE DELLA VALPOLICELLA Italy

A deliciously rich red wine with a dark chocolate and black cherry character, Amarone is made from grapes that have been left to dry in bunches after they have been harvested. It is high in alcohol and occasionally just off-dry.

Buying advice For the best quality examples, look for Classico on the label. For sweeter versions look for Recioto.
Food pairing Red meat and pasta with meat ragú.

Also try High-alcohol Zinfandel from California; sweet red wines from Banyuls in southern France.

6 PEDRO XIMÉNEZ SHERRY Spain

Also made from dried grapes, but with the addition of spirit (making it what is known as a fortified wine), PX sherry, as it is commonly known, is thickly syrupy and rich with fruit-cake flavours.

Buying advice Look for PX labelled VOS or VORS which are older versions with the greatest intensity and balance.
Food pairing Try pouring a glass over vanilla ice cream for a rich, alcoholic dessert.
Also try A similar wine is made from PX in nearby Montilla. Or try the less viscous and sweet but still indulgent Rutherglen Muscat from Australia.

175

Explore

How to Match Wine and Food

While wine is perfectly enjoyable on its own, it can really
come alive as part of a meal. However, just as some
ingredients don't taste good together, so not
every wine works with every kind of dish.

A few informal rules

There is a wealth of literature available about matching wine and food, and some people take it very seriously indeed. But it needn't be all that complex, and it certainly shouldn't be something to worry about. Indeed, the first rule of food and wine matching should always be: "If you like it, then it works."

However, most of us have experienced the sensation of jarring tastes. Just think about the last time you drank a glass of orange juice after cleaning your teeth: the mintiness in the toothpaste reacts horribly with all that acid in the orange juice. And while no wine-and-food match is ever that jarring, some can come close.

The key to avoiding this kind of reaction is to think about which are the most stongly flavoured components of the dish, and choose the wine accordingly. If a dish has lots of acidity, the wine will need to be sufficiently high in acidity, too; if it is sweet you'll need to find a wine with some sugar. The other thing to think about is flavour and texture: some matches work well because the wines have similar flavours to the food; others by making a contrast, again, just as they do in a recipe.

In this tasting we'll explore how different styles of wines interact with some common types of food. The idea is to experiment, see what you like, and come up with some rules of your own. The most important thing to remember is that food and wine matching is not a science, or even an art. It's simply about trying different combinations, and matching the food and wine to suit your personal taste. Have some fun with it!

Wine and cheese *is a classic flavour combination. But which wines will complement your cheese and which will overpower it, or be overpowered by it?*

Tasting Session

This is a fun tasting that works well if you want to put a twist on a dinner party. First of all, you'll need six wines, one for each of six popular styles. Then you'll need to pepare some food, one dish for each of the groups below. You only need a little per person.

1 FISH AND SEAFOOD
Something simple like grilled prawns or a light white fish, such as sole.

2 WHITE MEAT
Roast a chicken or some chicken legs in butter, salt, and herbs.

3 SPICY FOOD
Vegetable noodles cooked with chilli and coriander.

4 RED MEAT
A char-grilled steak or roast beef.

5 CHEESE
One blue, one creamy and white, and one hard yellow cheese.

6 DESSERT
An apple tart or tarte Tatin.

In this taste test the idea is to try each dish with each of the six wines. Start with the fish and move through the wines in the same order in which they appear over the next few pages. Remember, these are just suggestions of how the tastes and flavours work together. Taste is very much subjective, and one person's heavenly match can be another's gustatory hell.

Crisp dry white
Look for Fief Guérin Côte de Grandlieu Muscadet-Sur-Lie (see p.42); or William Fèvre Chablis

Rich dry white
Look for Sonoma Cutrer Sonoma Coast Chardonnay (see p.116); or Casa Lapostolle Cuvée Alexandra Chardonnay

"Classic wines to complement classic dishes, though personal taste will always be the ultimate arbiter."

Gently sweet white
Look for Maison Paul Zinck Alsace or Hugel Alsace Gewürztraminer (see p.75)

Fresh and fruity red
Look for Henry Fessy Côte de Brouilly (see p.53)

Rich and powerful red
Look for Tablas Creek Côtes de Tablas (see p.55); or Mondavi Cabernet Sauvignon Reserve Napa Valley

Rich sweet white
Look for Cyprès de Climens Sauternes (see p.46); or Les Lions de Suduiraut Sauternes

1 FISH AND SEAFOOD

Crisp dry white
This works beautifully. The crisp lemony acidity in the wine works like a squeeze of lemon, subtly enhancing the delicate flavours of the fish without overwhelming them, while the subtle fish allows the flavour of the wine to sing.

Rich dry white
Not bad. There's enough acidity here to act in a similar way to the crisp, dry white, but the oaky and buttery flavours are a little too powerful, and risk dominating rather than complementing a light fish dish.

Gently sweet white
The fish is completely overpowered here by the distinctive floral flavours, powerful body, and slight sugar sweetness.

This cod steak *and other light fish such as haddock, sole, or plaice work best with crisp, dry white.*

Fresh and fruity red
A surprisingly good match. Many people still believe that red wine cannot go with fish, but this style of wine's light tannins and brisk acidity actually work nicely, particularly if it is served well chilled at 10°C (50°F), which reduces the tannic impact. Would work better – like the rich, dry white – with a stronger flavoured fish.

Rich and powerful red
Oh dear. The strong tannins in this wine react with the fish oil to create an unpleasant metallic flavour.

Rich sweet white
No problem with acidity or tannin, but the powerful honeyed flavours and sweetness completely drown the delicate fish.

Prawns are a versatile seafood, *featuring in many international cuisines and types of dish.*

2 WHITE MEAT

Crisp dry white
Not a disaster. The acidity in the wine cuts through the fat of the meat and the butter, cleansing the mouth. However, that richness of flavour and fat often rather drowns out the delicate flavours in the wine.

Rich dry white
A great match of like with like. As with the crisp, dry white, there's acidity here to cut through the richness and clean the mouth, but it has more body and weight to carry off the fat, and the buttery flavours complement those of the dish.

Gently sweet white
A love-it-or-hate-it combination. The body and richness of both dish and wine are very much in sync, but there's less acidity in the wine to cut through the fat of meat. The aromatic qualities in the wine add either a welcome extra dimension (like a fruity condiment) or an unnecessary element (like a fruity condiment), depending on your personal preference.

Fresh and fruity red
Another good match. Again there is a cleansing acidity and with just enough body to match the weight and richness of the dish.

Rich and powerful red
Not a good match. The dish isn't rich enough to cope with the power and tannins in this style of wine, and the subtler flavours of the meat are drowned by the black fruit.

Rich sweet white
Not bad. The golden colour of the wine matches the golden hue of the chicken skin and, like the off-dry white, the sweetness and viscosity acts a little like a sweet condiment. Perhaps just a little too rich for the subtler chicken breast meat to shine.

Adding strong accompanying flavours *to your dish, such as citrus or garlic, can also affect how well it matches with your chosen wine.*

3 SPICY FOOD

Crisp dry white

The effect on the food is good. As with the fish dishes, the citrus acidity in this style of wine acts like a squeeze of lime. Lime is a common ingredient in southeast Asian cuisine, so the wine complements the dish. However, the effect of the food on the wine is not so good: the wine's subtle flavours are completely lost in the chilli heat.

Rich dry white

Not bad, but not brilliant. The tropical fruit flavours in the wine – pineapple or banana, for example – add a complementary touch, but once again it is hard to taste much of the wine through the overpowering heat of the chilli in the food.

Gently sweet white

A great match. The flavours of Gewürztraminer are almost Asian in themselves, with lychee, ginger, and galangal. But the crucial thing with this style of wine is the sugar, which masks and lessens the impact of the chilli. This is why palm sugar is such a popular ingredient in Thai food.

Fresh and fruity red

A definite no-go. In this combination, there are more problems with the chilli, which numbs the fruit flavours in the wine and accentuates its tannin and acidity instead. Not a pleasant match.

Rich and powerful red

A food-and-wine fight! That chilli heat again means you can't taste the wine's fruit, which, even more than the fresh and fruity red, leaves the wine tasting unpleasantly dry and tannic.

Rich sweet white

A good match, though not quite as intriguing as the off-dry white. There's plenty of sugar here too to balance the chilli, which means you can still taste the wine's fruit flavours. However, this style of wine's viscous texture can become a little too much if the food contains the subtler coriander leaf, another very common ingredient in this type of dish.

An Asian-style noodle dish *is often characterized by a strong chilli flavour as well as other flavours such as garlic, ginger, citrus, and coriander.*

4 RED MEAT

Crisp dry white
This match does no favours for the wine. Although the wine is refreshing enough to wash down the food, its subtle texture is lost in the wave of intense, fatty juice.

Rich dry white
Much better than the crisp, dry white. This style has enough body to cope with the fat in the meat. It's best if the wine (Chardonnay for example) has a bit of age, and has started to take on some savoury mushroom-like flavours, to complement the beef dish.

Gently sweet white
Another intriguing match. Like the rich dry white, this style of wine is sufficiently full-bodied to cope with the strong flavours and texture of the meat, but it can also add an intriguing element of Asian spice, setting off the beef like a ginger marinade.

Fresh and fruity red
A good match on a summer's day. There's just enough body and tannin in this style of wine for it not to be overwhelmed by the powerful meat flavours, and the racy acidity leaves the mouth feeling cleansed after all that fat.

Rich and powerful red
A classic match with which you may already be familiar from the local steak house. The fat in the roast meat bonds satisfyingly with the tannins in the wine, making the wine feel softer. The full dark fruity flavours in the wine echo those of the bloody steak.

For such a strong, meaty dish *beef matches surprisingly well with a wide range of wine styles, from the sweet to the dry.*

Rich sweet white
A traditional match that is rarely seen these days, because sweet wines are no longer as fashionable as they were a century ago. The match works best with roast beef when the meat is particularly well-hung and flavourful, the full-bodied viscous fruit matching the lusciously soft, rich meat.

5 CHEESE

Crisp dry white
Works very well with the soft cheese. Both the wine and the cheese have high acidity and delicate flavours. However, the blue cheese and the Cheddar are too strong and knock out the wine's delicate flavours.

Rich dry white
A good all-rounder. The rich dry white has enough acidity to cope with the soft, white cheese, and the oaky, buttery flavours echo those of the Cheddar very well. However, the blue cheese is just a touch too sharp and salty and overwhelms the wine.

Gently sweet white
Sweet/savoury match. Think of the sweet-and-savoury combination of cheese and pickle. This wine, with its slight sweetness, has the same effect, and enough body and richness to cope with a strong cheese.

Fresh and fruity red
Very good with cheese. Thanks to the high acidity, a fresh, fruity red can cope with the acidity of most of the cheeses.

Rich and powerful red
Not good. Big, powerful reds are high in tannin which jars horribly with the fat in the cheese, creating a metallic sensation.

Rich sweet white
Mixed success. A little too powerful for the soft cheese, the rich and sweet white comes into its own with the blue and hard cheese. There's enough acidity and body and the sweet fruit is a harmonious counterpoint.

A traditional cheese board *often contains a wide range of soft and hard cheeses, with a mixture of strong and subtle flavours.*

6 DESSERT

Crisp dry white
Oh no. The wine cannot cope with the strong flavours or the sweetness of the dessert, and seems listless and acidic.

Rich dry white
Not perfect, but better than the crisp, dry white. This match is very harmonious in terms of flavour – oak-aged Chardonnay has a similar buttery and fruity flavours to the tart, but the sugar in the dessert makes the wine feel too dry.

Gently sweet white
Better again. The richness and fruit quality match well (think of ginger-spiced apple). However, it isn't quite sweet enough – the sugar in the dessert makes even this wine feel a little harsh.

Fresh and fruity red
The sweet versus dry problem. Dry wines just taste harsh alongside sweet foods, and with red wines, a sweet food accentuates the tannin and acidity, too.

Rich and powerful red
Worse than the fresh fruity red! The sweetness of the tart simply emphasizes the tannins in the rich and powerful red, masking the fruit in the wine and making it feel astringent and unpleasant.

Apple-based desserts *balance sweet and acidic flavours, so wines of a similar character match best.*

Rich sweet white
A clear winner. It's no coincidence that this style of wine is known as a dessert wine. Only wines with comparable levels of sugar can hope to stand up to the sweet flavour of desserts. However, even dessert wines must also have decent acidity, otherwise the whole experience is just about the sweetness. In fact, a similar principle can be seen at work in the dessert itself: in an apple tart, the sugar is balanced by the apples' acidity.

Matching Food and Wine

The tables on these pages show at a glance some basic guidelines on which kinds of dishes usually work best with which wine style. That said, remember these are only suggestions; the most important guide to choosing the right wine is your own personal taste.

White Wine Styles

Food Type	Crisp & dry	Fruity & dry	Rich & dry	Gently sweet	Rich & sweet
Smoked	●●●	●●●		●	
Spicy		●		●●●	●●
Salty	●●●			●●	●●
Rich and creamy	●●	●●●		●●	●●
Light fish and shellfish	●●●	●●			
Meaty fish		●●	●●●	●	
Poultry			●●	●	●
Game					
Red meat				●	●
Stews and casseroles					
Hard cheese			●●●	●●	●●●
Blue cheese		●	●●	●●	●●●
Soft and creamy cheese	●●●			●	●
Grilled fish		●●●	●●	●	
Grilled meat			●●	●	●
Cold meat and charcuterie				●	
Vegetable dishes	●●	●●	●●	●●	
Pasta and pizza	●●		●●		
Egg dishes		●		●	
Desserts				●●	●●●

	Avoid	○○○	Good match	●●
	Acceptable	●○○	Great match	●●●

Red Wine Styles and Rosé

Food Type	Light & elegant /fresh & fruity	Smooth & fruity	Rich & powerful	Sweet & fortified	Rosé
Smoked	●●●	●●	○○○	○○○	●●
Spicy	●○○	●○○	○○○	○○○	●●
Salty	●●	○○○	○○○	●●	●●
Rich and creamy	●●●	○○○	○○○	○○○	●●
Light fish and shellfish	●●●	●○○	○○○	○○○	●●
Meaty fish	●●	○○○	○○○	○○○	●●
Poultry	●●●	●●●	○○○	○○○	●●
Game	○○○	●●	●●●	○○○	●○○
Red meat	●●●	●●●	●●●	●○○	●○○
Stews and casseroles	○○○	●●	●●●		
Hard cheese		●●●	●●	●●●	
Blue cheese	●○○			●●●	
Soft and creamy cheese	●●	●●	●●	●○○	●●
Grilled fish	●●●	●○○	○○○	○○○	●●●
Grilled meat	●●	●●●	●●	○○○	●●
Cold meat and charcuterie	●●	●●●	○○○	○○○	●●
Vegetable dishes	●●	●●	○○○	○○○	●●
Pasta and pizza	●●	●●●	○○○	○○○	●○○
Egg dishes	●○○	○○○	○○○	○○○	●○○
Desserts	○○○	○○○	○○○	●●	●○○

Index

About the Author

David Williams is the wine correspondent of the *Observer* newspaper, the deputy editor of the award-winning journal, *The World of Fine Wine*, and one of five members of the wine recommendation website, www.thewinegang.com. He has been writing about wine and wine-related matters for 15 years.

Acknowledgements

Photographic Credits
Dorling Kindersley would like to thank **Peter Anderson** for new photography. All images © Dorling Kindersley. For further information see www.dkimages.com

Author's Acknowledgements
Thanks to my family: Claudia, Raffy, and Mathilde.

Publisher's Acknowledgements
Dorling Kindersley would like to thank:

Bethan Davies at Waitrose Wine, Lucie Johnson at Gonzalez Byass UK Ltd, Nicola Lawrence at Liberty Wines, Alex Messis at W Communications, Kate Sweet at Limm PR, and Jason Yapp at Yapp Brothers for supplying bottles to photograph.

Leah Germann for producing the maps.

In the UK
Design assistance Joanne Doran, Vicky Read
Editorial assistance Helen Fewster, Holly Kyte
DK Images Claire Bowers, Freddie Marriage, Emma Shepherd, Romaine Werblow
Indexer Chris Bernstein

In India
Design assistance Ranjita Bhattacharji, Karan Chaudhary, Tanya Mehrotra
Editorial assistance Alka Thakur Hazarika
DTP Designer Arjinder Singh
CTS/DTP Manager Sunil Sharma